COUNTRY BLUES SONGBOOK

by Stefan Grossman, Stephen Calt and Hal Grossman

Oak Publications/New York
Music Sales Limited/London

PHOTOGRAPHS

Book Design by Jean Hammons and Mei Mei Sanford

© 1973 Oak Publications
33 West 60th Street
New York, New York 10023

Music Sales Limited
78 Newman Street
London, W1E 4JZ

Library of Congress Catalog Card Number 72-86652
International Standard Book Number 0-8256-0137-1

Contents

An Introduction

Blues at this point is many things to many different people. "Truth" is what you get a lot of when you ask somebody what blues is—"It's life." Which is something blues is. From the country blues there is a language of guitar and strings and pickings; from the city blues, a language of blues harp and blues piano. Which is also something blues is. And out of new blues bands, out of new blues sounds a free, endlessly renewing surge of blues melody. And that's something else blues is. So many things are blues— have become part of the blues—as a language, as an expression, as a consciousness. But at base, at essence, blues is song. Blues songs, all of them part of a language and style, are all of them uniquely and totally songs. Even in an instrumental, blues guitar or harp take only the part of the voice. The structure is still a song, the form is still a song. I think to begin with the blues you have to begin with this sense of what the blues is.

A song, by itself, is a distinct musical form—not like anything else. It is a text, *words*, set to a melody, and in the relationship between the two words take on the shape of melody and the melody begins to have the emotional force of the words. Blues, as song, isn't like any form of song. It is at its essence not guitar styles, not a certain number of measures, not a sequence of chords, but only song.

A group of blues songs, like this one, in one way doesn't give a clear sense of one of the things about the blues that is different from other kind of songs. These are great blues songs, with melodic lines shaped to great blues verses. In most blues, though, and for most singers, words are much more important than melody. Many singers go through their entire careers as musicians using three or four melodies, sometimes even one or two. They simply write new sets of words. Most singers don't even seem to think in terms of writing a melody; the melodic part of it is a kind of given, as in a mathematical problem. The sense of writing a new blues comes from the words—an idea in a line of phrase, sometimes something personal, sometimes just something out of the general run of blues lyrics.

Even when it comes to going to the studio to get some of it down on record, it's still the words that are the center of it. When you went into a studio with Otis Spann or with Furry Lewis, the man usually got out a much folded piece of paper with new words written on it. Then when each started singing the melody was always something familiar. The strength of blues is that in these little handwritten sets of words, a new idea for a blues or a reworking of an old blues idea, music takes a new strength, a new uniqueness.

The melodic material of blues is so clear in its forms that someday probably an academician will be able to do a theme classification and put all blues melodies into three or four main classes. I did an informal survey of blues melody, and of 259 blues I listened to there were 191 with a similar melodic line, twenty of them with a partly spoken variation on the same line, 8 of them used the same country dance melody, and only 12 of them could be said to have a melody that was used only for its own text. So in blues song, except for these unusual pieces, it isn't a melody that's the concern.

For many blues the text isn't distinctive either. As Furry Lewis described his own ways of writing,

> "The first verse could be the last. You know, just any old verse that I wanted I could make that the first, then go right on from there and just rhyme up from it and make them all kind of match, you know."

There will probably be the same kind of academic classification of blues verses. Unlike almost any other kind of song it is an entire verse that's used to work from—so the verse has to be the place to start with any study of blues words.

There have been, literally, thousands of blues recorded in the last fifty years, an incredibly rich treasure of a people's experience—or that part of it they were permitted to sing. In so many areas it's so rich we still haven't measured what's there, what's still to be heard there. Going through some old tapes I suddenly found myself listening to an unissued Mercy Dee Walton blues from the 1950's that was as raw and pure as the first blues that came out of the Southern countryside in the 1920's. In this richness of blues there are songs, some of the greatest songs to be composed by anyone in this century. Some of them are in this book—a beginning, an opening to the blues as song. Since that's what the blues is, if you do want to come close to the experience of blues, it's the best place there is to start.

—Samuel Charters
Saltsjö Boo, Sweden

Dedicated to Israel Young

Preface

This book has been a joy to put together. It was fun to choose those tunes we thought presented the most interesting musical expression as well as lyric content from thousands of recorded blues. It was very encouraging to have people all over the world contribute ideas, photographs, and miscellaneous data. Hopefully the result will please you and open up several new doors.

It was not an easy task to pick all the tunes. We were hindered by the mammoth publishers who somehow controlled some of the old blues. They tended to be uncooperative in seeing their material presented. One got the impression that these companies would rather see songs gather dust in files. Other publishers were of help. Our special love and thanks go to Wynwood Music and Peter Kuykendall, Tradition Music and Chris Strachweiz, Sondick Music and Dick Waterman, and Uncle Doris Music and Mike Vernon. These people have helped to make this project a reality.

We only hope this book will show better the world of the Country Blues. We include songs from Mississippi John Hurt, Mance Lipscomb, Furry Lewis and Robert Wilkins to the hard Delta Blues of Robert Johnson, Charlie Patton and Son House. The strange textures of Skip James and King Solomon Hill and Bukka White stand right next to the Texas Blues of Lil Son Jackson and Lightning Hopkins. This is a book that shows the grand cross-section of the Country Blues.

My special thanks to Sam Charters for his help, and to Stephen Calt, and to Hal Grossman who introduces the blues form in a way we can understand. This is more than an ordinary songbook. It holds documentation of a sociological movement as well as a music form.

Lastly my thanks to Jean Hammons and Herb Wise.

I hope you enjoy.
Peace,
Stefan Grossman

The Country Blues As Meaning

To the poor and subject man a tongue has been given.

Theognis

With the possible exception of jazz, whose cult literature has served as a clearing-house for cliché blues criticism, no form of pop or folk music has been so volitized by gaseous generalities as blues. While the overall diversity of rock or pop music is ordinarily taken for granted even by the worst of its respective critics, blues gets glibly explained in terms of a single all-embracing message, the precise meaning of which is subject to vary according to the preoccupations and prejudices of the particular writer who broaches the subject. But whether blues is ultimately regarded as a statement of despair (which has always been the most popular platitude applied to it), a genre of poetry, an "intensely personal" vehicle of self-expression, or as an oral chronicle of black byways, the yawning dimensions of the critical claim made on its behalf remain the same.

It is not because country blues is so broad in scope that such criticism flounders, but rather because the form has less intellectual and social significance than its devotees would have it. The preoccupation with blues as meaning has fatally obscured its original function as entertainment. To its contemporary audience of Southern blacks, country blues served as a passing diversion, a pleasurable escape from the very realities it is now held to express. There is some question that the blues song had any abstract meaning in and of itself.[1] The vast majority of country blues recorded in the 1920s (when the music had its greatest commercial value) does not offer a cohesive theme or subject for modern scrutiny, let alone express a discernable attitude or opinion. The fleeting nature of the actions and sentiments they tend to express thwarts schematic interpretation of blues verse. At most, country blues presents a set of conventions to the would-be commentator, and these conventions bear witness less to the meaning of the genre than to its simple redundancy. It would be almost accurate to say that country blues has no intrinsic nature, only a history. But this history itself is so obscure that one cannot know how most blues performers actually understood their songs, what the various idiomatic expressions *(bullfrog blues, mamlish blues)* that abound in the lyrics were supposed to have meant, or who the composers of the most commonplace blues couplets were in the first place. As one might expect of an art form that is nebulous enough to make instant specialists of its listeners, these inconveniences but little perturb the venerable blues authority. Instead of recoiling from the vagaries of country blues, he blusters onwards with the smugness of the evangelist with whom he shares complete disregard for the nuances of source criticism and textual analysis. To lend a gloss of authority to the salesmanship that underlies most of blues scholarship, the sociology text serves as Book of Revelations.

As a tool to expose the essence of country blues, the social sciences have a double-edged dullness. Far from being merely boring, most of the black sociology contemporary with country blues (a form that flourished roughly from around the turn of the century until around the Second World War) was also elitist, didactic, and not at all concerned with black secular music. Until comparatively recent times sociological studies of black culture have been little more than a scoreboard to measure the performance of blacks against middle-class American value systems that had already rejected blacks out of hand. With Babbitt's boldness, the sociologist thus ignored blues entirely. Only the spiritual which testified to the moral purity of blacks was accorded any social or artistic validity.[2] Thus today, some thirty

---

[1] By responding to the inevitable question "What is blues?" with a rote definition of the word itself rather than of the musical form, the country bluesman helps perpetuate the illusion that "Blues is a worried mind."

[2] Even the prestigious studies of DuBois and Myrdal reflect this attitude.

years after country blues passed out of favor as a form of black entertainment, the researcher can draw few conclusions about blues' relationship to its environment.

As for the class of plantation blacks who created the genre long before the phrase "country blues" was ever invoked to describe their efforts, they shall have to be reinvented, for they had no discernable existence except as a quaint curiosity to readers of dialect literature or a social problem to buttress the sociology tract. As human beings they interested practically nobody; the minds of rural blacks being considered devoid of thought. One of the Twenties' foremost academic authorities on the South, Ulrich B. Phillips, held that "A field negro lives in a kind of perpetual doze, a dreary haze . . ." When the great Mississippi flood of 1927 left thousands of black sharecroppers homeless in the Mississippi Delta, the *New York Times'* most penetrating comment on the victims was: ". . . probably three-fourths of them are negroes, the best type of the old-time Southern 'darky' such as Joel Chandler Harris and Thomas Nelson Page immortalized." [1]

From the bleak surface evidence of sociology, the lives of Southern blacks during the blues era were too blighted to allow for their creation of a music with the strange longevity of country blues, a commodity which has survived the very sociological stereotypes that long ostracized it. For the most part, however, these same lives were untrammeled by all but the most rudimentary outside inquiry. To be sure, the privately-owned plantations and backwater Southern towns that once spawned country bluesmen often figured in the travelogues that were so popular during the nineteenth century (but had fallen out of fashion, alas, by the 1920s). [2] With rare exceptions, the sightseer viewed the Southern black through the eyes of his local white guides, if he saw him at all. In 1903 DuBois was able to write of black people:

> . . . how little we really know of these millions,—of their daily lives and longings, of their homely joys and sorrows, or their real shortcomings and the meaning of their crimes! All this we can only learn by intimate contact with the masses, and not by wholesale arguments covering millions separate in time and space, and differing widely in training and culture. [3]

The caste, class and cultural barriers that isolated plantation blacks from the rest of society precluded such intimacy. The most earnest of those who consorted with these largely detested people were apt to find them pitiable or perplexing. Booker T. Washington was sometimes taken aback by what he termed the "peculiar mental processes" of country blacks, though he was not above telling a joke at their expense. The opaqueness of country blacks nonplussed Delta planter Alfred Stone, a pragmatic gentleman farmer who was conversant with the writings of DuBois at a time when Washington was considered the "proper" black spokesman and who consented to capitalize "Negro" four decades before the *Times* decreed that spelling fit to print. Speaking of the black sharecropper before the American Economic Society in 1901, Stone declared flatly: "His mental processes are past finding out, and he cannot be counted on to do or not to do a given thing under given circumstances."

This alleged racial inscrutability seems to have been an article of faith among genteel Mississippi whites; en route to Harvard, Faulkner's Quentin Compson reflected thusly on blacks: "They came into white people's lives like that in sharp black trickles . . . the rest of the time just voices that laugh when you see nothing to laugh at, tears when no reason for tears." [4] The Delta's "poet laureate" William Alexander Percy saw them as "a people

1 *The New York Times*: April 26, 1927: p. 6
2 The local color account provides our only glimpse into nineteenth century black music. As history documents these accounts are too incidental, too vague, and too amateurish to be definitive, the oft-quoted rhapsodies of Fannie Kemble and Lafcadio Hearn notwithstanding.
3 *The Souls Of Black Folk*: Avon Library: New York: 1969: p. 302.
4 *The Sound And The Fury*: Random House: New York: 1946: p. 189.

deceptively but deeply alien and unknowable."[1] Indeed, the only pundits able to divine the psyche of the old-fashioned rural black appear to have been the unvarnished Southern bigot, who always prided himself a specialist on "nigger nature", and the latter-day blues expert, whose infallible intuition enables him to explain the one art form intrinsic to that group as a revelation of its innermost workings. The naivety of all blues criticism that assumes such guileless transparency on the part of the blues artists is no less unsettling than its well-intentioned arrogance. For to seriously entertain the notion that blacks freely unburdened themselves in blues song also requires the belief that they enjoyed freedom of speech under the Jim Crow regime. The suitability of country blues sentiment from the standpoint of this regime is obvious enough from the Southern planter's readiness to engage artists for his own parties.[2] Moreover, the white floorwalker was a common fixture within the sawmill, levee camp, and plantation barrelhouse that frequently served as the site of blues performances for black audiences.

Like the white Southerner who once generalized about the black race from the example of the so-called "plantation darky" or "folk Negro" (the polite equivalent employed by Fisk sociologist Charles S. Johnson), the audacious blues critic is wont to unblinkingly perceive the country blues that spoke ambiguously on behalf of one black social stratum in terms of the entire race. Most of the clichés that have been perpetuated about black song since the nineteenth century have only mimicked prevailing attitudes towards that sociological abstraction, "the Negro". When it was fashionable to dismiss blacks as quaint primitives, so was their music generally considered frivolous and barbaric. Today, in keeping with white noblesse oblige, blues music is invariably patronized, no matter how atrocious. The critics of each age endow black song with the qualities they hold desirable for black people. Much was once made of the "unfailing good humor" displayed by black folk song and the singer's supposed amusement at his own foibles. Of late the blues that are contemporary with such pronouncements have come to signify anger or protest. Yet throughout such shifts in critical wind the country bluesman has understood a single obligation: to make himself enjoyable to every audience, be it the foxtrotting planter of yesteryear or the sedentary concert-goer of recent vintage.

The real extent of the blues' appeal to the black audience remains a matter of conjecture. Both the view of the country bluesman as a racial spokesman and the conception of his work as folk music imply an unqualified community acceptance that is far from evident to those hapless blues historians who actually scour the former haunts of musicians in an attempt to elicit some memory of them. A complete indifference to the blues party marked the responses of a thousand black Detroiters, all fresh arrivals from the South, who were interviewed in the Twenties on the subject of their recreational habits: fishing, sitting down, doing nothing, and attending lodge meetings numbered among favorite activities.[3] Several years later Charles S. Johnson's study of country blacks, *Growing Up In The Black Belt*, relegated the bluesman and his audience to the lowest of the six class categories by which he divided the Southern black. Although Johnson's social pyramiding was in itself somewhat dubious,[4] there is no question but that blues was always somewhat disreputable even among its Saturday night following, the bluesman being a favorite scapegoat of the following morning's sermon. By now the question of the country bluesman's popularity or even respectability is merely academic: for the past thirty years neither city nor country blues have had any currency as a popular art among blacks. Their present listening audience is almost exclusively white. It was with white acclamation that country blues first gained respectability, or

1 *Lanterns On The Levee*: Knopf: New York: 1941: p. 298.
2 For all anybody knows, there may be justice in a planter's remark to me that the bluesmen of his acquaintance were "what we used to call white men's niggers."
3 Forester B. Washington: "Recreational Facilities For The Negro": *The Annals Of The American Academy of Political and Social Science*: November 1928: p. 272.
4 He considered criminality and immorality a social category unto itself.

even respect. Were it not for posthumous white patronage, a name like Charlie Patton would be synonymous with nothing, rather than with the Mississippi Delta blues tradition to which he so richly contributed. And when a chorus of white blues critics pontificates on country bluesman's stirring protest against white racism, they are chiefly amusing themselves. Black attention is diverted elsewhere. Given current black antipathies, the very spectre of white blues enthusiasm creates the outline of the handkerchief head, and the few black commentators who salute the blues as part of black heritage are left in the unenviable position of parroting white criticism.

So much for the country blues artist as a folk or race hero. As a historical personage he will probably never come into perspective despite the best efforts of the blues biographer. The only remaining grounds on which one can approach country blues is aesthetic, but nearly all of the generalities that could conceivably be applied to blues as art (including those of this essay) would be pedantic in character. As a musical form, blues is far less susceptible to dogmatic textbook analysis than the classical ragtime pioneered by Scott Joplin, for its inventors (unlike Joplin and his counterparts) were the products of a society that was completely innocent of abstract notions of music or poetry. Whether or not this innocence was a form of grace (one shudders at the thought of country bluesmen creating conventional pop music) it remains true that the concise definitions of blues framed by academicians were not inflexible laws first conceptualized by the artists themselves, but merely conventions they acquired by osmosis and came to intuitively observe (or disregard). Similarly, it would seem that in versifying the country blues artist did not work from specific notions as to what distinguished *good* from *bad* lyrics.

It is not even clear that the musicians we have come to call country bluesmen (a term unknown to them) had a clear notion as to what they considered a blues. It is doubtful that blues originally signified anything beyond a secular dance tune, as distinct from the spiritual. The artist who happened to reflect on the meaning of his work would be likely to draw the unremarkable conclusion (considering the nomenclature of his song) that it was sad in character, or that it told a "true" story about life. He would be less likely to shape his material to meet these specifications, although there is a standard litany of blues woes. If the country bluesman ever mulled over the musical aspects of blues he might have thought to contrast it to an even fuzzier category he called ragtime, a word he sometimes used to characterize uptempo pieces.[1]

From its inception country blues was a performing rather than a compositional art. So long as a particular work found an audience willing to subsidize its performance, it had fulfilled its intended function. In keeping with his utilitarian outlook the bluesman used his verses by various turns to agreeably impress the listener with his wit, worldly wisdom, sexual irresistability, or pitiable quality. His most strenuous flagellations of the opposite sex may come only as a ruse. Indeed, the late Mississippi bluesman Skip James fancied the power of country blues verse to make mush of its ostensible targets as one of its prime virtues:

> . . . You take some girl out there: perhaps she have misused you. The first thing she says, she hear you play: "Oh, is that him? Boy, it was somethin'. . . I've got to go back and apologize with him . . . We got to have this thing talked over again."
>
> . . . Now that blues done hit her . . . And she feels then, them blues done struck her so hard like that, her life will be a void without my presence . . . She'll follow me as long as I'm in hearin' distance . . .

---

1 There is no connection between ragtime as understood by country bluesmen and the Scott Joplin variety, which the classical ragtime historian David Jasen defines as "a continuous syncopation of the melodic strain harmonized with an even, steady rhythm."

perhaps she gonna make herself available until I may approach her again.[1]

Even when a blues song reaped no such bonanzas (perhaps it never did) its performance was nearly always parlayed into immediate tangible assets: money, drinks, food, free train rides. In confining circumstances the musicians even won pardons through their blues-playing ability, or so they sometimes brag.[2] It requires no Skinnerian psychologist to see a fundamental impetus behind country blues-playing in such acts of positive reinforcement, particularly in view of the great deprivations suffered by the rural black. The former record salesman H.C. Speir, who was perhaps the only white talent scout to attend blues parties in the South, recalled his discoveries Charlie Patton and Tommy Johnson to researcher Gayle Wardlow: "Their blues-singing was brought about more or less I would say by . . . being poor; singing blues would make money, understand."

The monetary windfalls netted by country bluesmen did not come without their own price. No artist with the ability to pull in the weekly wages of a Mississippi sharecropper over a one night's stint in a dance-hall (and this is reckoning it modestly) was cut out to win any popularity contests among the less fortunate males of his class. The country bluesman's popularity with his own sex appears to have been inversely proportional to his popularity with his female clientele. The frontier ambience that figures in probable blues ancestors like *Bob McKinney* and *Railroad Bill* continued to reverberate through the blues party of the Twenties, often to the discomforture of the bluesman. ". . . You get on these plan'ations," Skip James once observed, "some of these guys had pretty good influence with 'ole boss', and they'd just soon kill you as not . . . A few country peoples that was around a guitar-player had just common jealousy." But whether he enjoyed fraternal or acrimonious relations with his non-musical counterparts, the country bluesman was first and foremost a tradesman concerned not with the metaphysics that fill up blues treatises but with the simple business at hand. A close associate of Charlie Patton's told Gayle Wardlow of their stolid routine: "We could get ready to go on to a dance; first thing we wanna do is get us a drink or two, and we would be playin'. We never did talk about, you know . . . people or life: we just playin' . . ."

The career of the typical country blues musician seems to have been a ritual of recapitulation rather than a progression of continuous development or change. To revise musical motifs that had managed to find favor with a given audience or to discard pieces of proven popularity seems to have been exceptional for him. Likewise, the artist who revamped his lyrics for the sake of greater timeliness or even cogency was anomalous, judging from the internal evidence of blues songs. The artist who fully created his own lyrics to begin with was a decided misfit, swamped by competitors who were never stigmatized for simply parroting or paraphrasing blues verses already in circulation. The outstanding attribute of the country blues lyric is its eclectic quality; so much verse overlapping exists among recorded blues that one can never safely regard a particular song as the original composition of the artist with whom it is associated.[3] Rarely are the lyrics deployed by the country blues performer anywhere as distinctive as his guitar style.

It is by no means established that the general body of verses that emerged from country blues recordings of the Twenties were first created by professional entertainers. The folklorist Newman White collected dozens of couplets between 1915-1916 from the unaccompanied songs of farm-

---

1 Unless otherwise indicated, this and other quotations from blues artists have been transcribed verbatim from taped interviews with the author.
2 It is also said that such artists as Tommy Johnson and George (Bullet) Williams were pardoned from jail in the same fashion, by reducing their captors to tears with musical performances like *Poor Boy Long Ways From Home.*
3 To call the most jaded country blues verses "traditional" is to overlook the premium artists themselves placed on an originality they often failed to realize, and to euphemize this very unoriginality. No "tradition" ever ordained a given set of blues verses or subject matter, only convention.

hands, miners, domestics and the like that prove virtually identical with recorded country blues couplets of the following decade. That a majority of these songs were heard within a single locale (the small hamlet of Auburn, Alabama) conclusively demonstrates the ubiquity of country blues verse. Whether it also argues for the transmission of such verse from the folk amateur to the professional bluesman (or vice-versa) is a moot point: meticulous scholar that he was, White shared the folklorists' finicky aversion to blues as a decadent commercial development and completely overlooked the possible implications of his research.

In the absence of contemporary inquiry into the sources of blues or any kindred form of black folk song[2], it is impossible to either date or assign authorship to the most familiar country blues couplets. Some verses regurgitated by the singers clearly predate the birth of country blues as a genre, an event that might have taken place anytime over the last two decades of the nineteenth century, if not within the first decade of the twentieth. The oldest discernible couplet used by a country bluesman occurs as the opening verse of Charley Jordan's 1930 recording, *Keep It Clean*: *I went to the river, I couldn't get across; I jumped on your pappy 'cause I thought he was a horse*. A precursor of the same couplet appeared in the original published version of *Jump Jim Crow*, the prototypical minstrel song popularized by "Daddy" Rice in the 1840s and partly derived by the same singer from black sources in the 1820s. (The stanza in question had a parallel existence in a ballad and nursery rhyme of the nineteenth century.) Another blues throwback to minstrelsy is the standard verse: *Some folks say that a preacher won't steal; I caught two in my cornfield*. An earlier rendition of this verse (identifying a "nigger" as the culprit) was printed as part of a minstrel song in 1854.[3]

The oldest known country blues verse of unquestionable black authorship forms the title lyric of Bo Carter's *Who's Been Here?*, recorded in 1940: *Baby, who's been here since your daddy been gone? Well it musta been a preacher, baby, he had a derby on*. A slave song quoted in the 1855 autobiography of a freedman began: *Who's been here since I've been gone? Pretty little gal wid a josey on*. A verse Lafcadio Hearn collected from the singing of Cincinatti roustabouts and published in 1870 cropped up in Tommy McClennan's 1939 blues best-seller, *Bottle Up And Go*: *Nigger and a white man playing Seven Up; White man played the ace, and the nigger feared to take it up*.

Despite the long-held (and basically unsupportable) belief that country blues evolved directly from the "field hollers" once sung by black sharecroppers, few country blues verses are cast in the recognizable mode of a work song. An exception that demonstrates the antiquity of some blues couplets is the title phrase of Robert Johnson's 1936 recording, *Last Fair Deal Gone Down*: *It's the last fair deal gone down . . . on that Gulfport Island Road*. The song undoubtedly pertains to the construction of the Gulf and Ship Island Railroad in southern Mississippi between 1887-1902.[4] A work song of similar vintage probably occasioned a stanza the Georgia bluesman Peg Leg Howell recorded in 1929: *The longest train that I ever seen; Run 'round Joe Brown's coal mine*. Howell's verse is a seeming carryover from the 1880s, when Georgia's four-time governor Joseph Emerson Brown (1821-1894) operated the Dade Coal Company with the assistance of black convict labor donated by magnanimous state officials.

A one-liner W.C. Handy once recalled hearing a bottleneck guitarist perform near the turn of the century at a Tutwiler, Mississippi railroad depot is the earliest blues stanza that can be related to a blues performance as such.

1 Until the publication of Sam Charters' *Country Blues* (1959), all blues were generally considered the off-spring of W.C. Handy (1873-1958), a heady blunder since Handy's own memory of blues melody (though he did not consider it such) went back to 1892.
2 Comporting themselves like Freudian analysts, folklorists of the Twenties remained aloof from the singers who provided them with free associated verse.
3 For this and the succeeding example, cf. Newman White: *American Negro Folk Songs*: Folklore Associates reprint of the 1928 edition: Hatboro, Pa: 1965.
4 In 1925, when Johnson was a mere teen-ager, the line reverted to the Illinois Central.

The much-fabled lyric, *Goin' where the Southern cross the Dog*, commemorated the then-recent construction of the Y&MV ("Dog") railroad in the Mississippi Delta. At the time Handy heard it sung any traveler leaving Tutwiler by rail was inevitably headed "where the Southern cross the Dog"; the first stop out of Tutwiler, the town of Moorhead forty miles southwards, was also a way station along the Southern line running between Greenville, Mississippi and Birmingham.[1] With the subsequent completion of the Y&MV, the Southern crossed the Dog in four different Delta towns. The notion nevertheless persisted among Delta blues singers that Moorhead formed the junction of the Southern and the "Dog". Folk ingenuity must have risen to new heights once the Delta branch of the Southern gave way to another railroad in the late 1920s, thus robbing the song chestnut of its last semblance of realism. At least one Delta bluesman who continued using it was unfazed by this rude development; according to his etymology, "Goin' where the Southern cross the Dog" evoked the southern branch of the "Dog". "We didn't hardly never say nothin' about the *south* 'Dog'," he told Gayle Wardlow, "we called it the 'southern'. The 'southern' cross the 'Dog' in Moorhead."[2]

The country bluesman's conservative habit of clinging to familiar couplets long after they had lost their topicality or novelty would have by no means detracted from his crowd appeal. His audience had been weaned on spirituals and songs like *Make Me A Pallet On The Floor* or *Stack O'Lee*, all of which came with built-in tunes and texts. As for the bluesman himself, he was hired not for his poesy but on the basis of his ability to animate a dance audience, unless he plied his wares in the street.[3] However it may have been idealized, originality in verse was practically unattainable over the course of a performance he was obliged to maintain so long as his audience kept its feet. Nor could it have mattered if dozens of other artists in different locations were capitalizing on precisely the same material. The introduction of blues on phonograph brought a new emphasis to blues lyrics, if only because a passive rather than participatory audience now awaited them. That the country bluesman who obtained recording sessions in the middle and latter Twenties were so often unequal to the challenge of the new medium that would reap dividends for facile songwriters like Leroy Carr and Barbecue Bob is probably indicative of the fact that they could not have realistically anticipated their discovery by commercial talent scouts. But by the same token many country bluesmen made only a hack's response to the novelty presented by the blues recording, copying its verses as they came down to him. Remonstrated by Son House for this practice, the legendary Robert Johnson is said to have replied: "So what? Who's gonna know the difference?" Probably the country bluesman never lived whose muse was not expediency.

Because the country bluesman's expediency so often took the form of imitation the idea that his songs are sheer self-expression has no real foundation beyond their first-person premise, a convention probably adopted from the *Book of Psalms*.[4] It is true that the country blues artist will commonly claim an autobiographical basis for his songs, but this explanation probably draws its sails less from true projection than from a profound distrust of the imagination that rejects anything remotely fanciful. Some of the song imagery the country bluesmen seem to personalize strikes his present-day listener as original simply because it is so hoary as to have passed beyond cultural memory. Such is true of the title lyric of *Cypress Grove Blues*, which Skip James liked to explain as the outgrowth of his experience as a timber-cutter in Mississippi: *I would rather be buried in some cypress*

1 Cf. *The Journal Of The Western Society Of Engineers*: October 22, 1902: Chicago.
2 But for the bluesman's own preoccupation with the literal, and a critic's insistence that "every coloured hobo understands" the above verse, its historical basis would be of no concern to any commentator.
3 Both Skip James and Son House even went so far as to say that this audience showed no real interest in blues lyrics.
4 The Bible was the basic reading matter of the poorly-educated black Southerner, and the *Book of Psalms* a well-spring for spiritual refrains.

grove; Than to have some woman, Lord' that I can't control. The sentiment behind this verse was lifted from *Proverbs* 21:19, which states: "It is better to dwell in the wilderness, than with a contentious and an angry woman." Cypress has served as a symbol of death and burial since antiquity, and was so employed as an allusion by Horace, Shakespeare, Milton, and Poe. Its symbolism had grown so hackneyed by the nineteenth century that Flaubert's *Dictionary Of Platitudes* would snort that cypress "grows only in graveyards."

From an impulse more obscure than the bluesman's own, his critic is even more guilty of resurrecting cultural clichés as intimate personal disclosures. On the basis of such songs as *Hellhound On My Trail* and *Stones In My Passway* a whole literature has sprung up around Mississippi's Robert Johnson (1912?-1938), consisting solely of turgid pronouncements like: ". . . the byroads of despair and anxiety and rejection . . . were the sole markers of his demon-driven journey through life . . ." Although Johnson can no longer answer to the meaning of his songs, it would be no surprise if he indeed envisioned hellhounds on his trail, though the phrase itself stemmed from a previous recording by "Funny Paper" Smith. A proverbial specimen, the hellhound seems to have been a plantation equivalent of the flying saucer. It had a long history in religious superstition before first terrorizing (if not titillating) the black populace. Perhaps thinking of Cerberus, Luther invoked the "hound of hell" in a sixteenth century sermon. Burton believed the devil could assume the shape of a black dog; the hellhounds unleashed in Shakespeare's *Tempest* were given the power to cause convulsions, "shortened sinews", and "pinch-spots" in their victims. The eighteenth century English peasant sometimes stumbled upon these wonders in his favorite blasted heath; the local strain, known as the "heath hound", travelled in packs supposedly hand-picked by Satan from the dead souls of unbaptized infants.[1]

Mississippi blacks interviewed by the folklorist Newbell Niles Puckett during the first two decades of this century told of seeing ghosts in the form of dogs, bearing gleaming red eyes and calf-sized bodies. It would seem that these visitants signified mortal sin on the part of the beholder:

> I seen or dreamed something. I thought I saw some dogs, some lean hounds, and I thought that meant old Satan was running me. So I knew I'd better get religion . . .[2]

> I saw the Devil when I was praying to get religion. He struck my track, and he ran me in the field. He looked just like an old hound dog . . . The Devil's got a pack of hounds and he'll chase you.[3]

Johnson's *Stones In My Passway* is similarly indebted to the religious vocabulary of the folk penitent; the basis of its "intensely personal" disclosure (*I've got stones in my passway, and my road seems dark as night*) is the third chapter of the *Book of Lamentations*: "He hath led me and brought me into darkness . . . He hath enclosed my ways with hewn stone, he hath made my paths crooked." An ancient proverb recorded by Mencken holds that "the way of sinners is made plain with stones . . ." while an antebellum Negro spiritual begins: *Old Satan is one busy old man; He rolls dem blocks all in my way . . .*

Only a smattering of the figurative phrases found in country blues appear to have been coined by the musicians themselves. More often than not he makes use of the so-called "dead metaphor" or the stock colloquialism of the nineteenth century in order to make a figurative statement.[4] Unless one fancies the country bluesman a poet his reliance upon established idioms is nothing fraudulent, but merely evidence of the fact that he

---

1 Bayne-Powell: *English Country Life In The Eighteenth Century*: John Murray: London: 1937: pp. 272-273.
2 Charles S. Johnson: *Growing Up In The Black Belt*: Shocken reprint of the 1941 edition: New York: 1967, p. 160.
3 Richard M. Dorson: *American Negro Folktales*: Fawcett Publications: Greenwich, Conn.:1967, p. 264.
4 From the platitude of asking for bread and receiving stones (cited in Partridge's *Dictionary of Cliches*), Tommy Johnson apparently arrives at the blues statement: "I asked for water, gimme gasoline."

sang conversationally and thus possessed the modest phrase-making abilities of the average speaker.

He also had a decidedly limited capacity to visualize, or so his pictorial images would indicate. But often these derivative images are so skillfully woven into the artist's own dialect as to convey a strong flavor of originality: he finds paraphrase more agreeable than parrotry. To the ballad proposition that *If young women could swim like fishes in the water; There's many a young man would strip and swim after*, the Mississippi bluesman offers this equivalent: *If I was a catfish, swimmin' down in the deep blue sea, I would have these good-lookin' women, fishin' after me*. A basic prop of the traditional ballad appears to set the stage for Charlie Patton's famous departure in *Pony Blues*: *Hitch up my pony, saddle up my black mare, I'm gonna find a rider, baby, in the world somewhere*. Centuries earlier, the balladeer had implored: *O saddle to me my milk-white steed; And go fetch my pony, O! That I might ride and seek my bride. . . ."*

To depict the blues, Patton is cued by the imagery of *Psalm 72*, which prophesies that God "shall come down like rain upon the mown grass; as showers that water the earth." He sings: *Took my baby, to meet the mornin' train, And the blues came down, baby, like showers of rain*.[1] The heavenly retribution of *Psalm 78* that "destroyed their vines with hail and their sycamore trees with frost" blights Blind Lemon Jefferson no less than the Israelite: *No more potatoes, this frost has killed the vine, Well the blues ain't nothin' but a good woman on your mind*.

Despite the critical cliché that the country bluesman lived close to nature, he is able to furnish few if any original naturalistic images or comparisons. When Son House sings: *My black mama's face shines like the sun* he is probably not depicting the visible glow of some girl-friend but reaching into the *Book of Matthew*, which informs him that "The righteous shine as the sun." As an ex-neighbor of that artist told Gayle Wardlow: "He knowed two things: he knowed the blues and he knowed the Bible." House would also seem to have known pop song. His 1942 Library of Congress recording, *Low Down Dirty Dog Blues* begins: *You know the sun is going down, I say behind that old western hill, You know I wouldn't do a thing, not against my baby's will*. A gratuitous sunset likewise marks the opening of the mushy epic, *Deep Purple* (1934): *The sun is sinking low behind the hill, I loved you long ago, I love you still*. It is apparently also in recollection of pop song that House suffers one of those "intensely personal" griefs so dear to our critic in *My Black Mama*: *I got a letter this mornin' how do you think it read? "Oh hurry, hurry, the gal you love is dead."* In an old tear-jerker called *The Letter Edged In Black* the postman personally delivers the same sad tidings: *. . . I took the letter from him, then I broke the seal and this is what it said: ". . . Come right home my boy, your dear old mother's dead."*

To the extent that such incidental blues borrowings are symptomatic the simplistic notion of blues as "a Negro experience"[2] obviously stands in need of revision. In its present state of development, country blues source criticism is no more than a sniper facing a hydra-headed army of couplets. At best it can claim a single corpse. The stage manipulations that become so evident in country blues verse should finally lay to rest the ludicrous but still-lingering scenario of the artist turning to song as a means of articulating his personal woes. Whether the thoroughly stylized griefs projected in blues verse are heartfelt or fanciful, the dramatic pretense of "having the blues" nevertheless pays homage to a sensibility so dated that the very word "blues" currently suggests the song form and nothing else.

Popular wisdom that perished only with the nineteenth century has generally viewed the profession of sorrow as more becoming than mirth, and it is in keeping with the dated world view of the country bluesman that

---

1 By contrast, Robert Johnson's image of "blues fallin' down like hail" forms a proverbial comparison of the nineteenth century.
2 Leroi Jones: *Blues People*: William Morrow and Company: New York: 1963: p. 94.

Skip James invoked Scriptural authority for his own blues-singing: "What the blues is, a lot of people don't consider; don't know what they is. But I style it like this . . . in *Psalms*, the Bible states that a person can be blue; have the blues." Not only does the *Old Testament* sanction sorrow, but sanctifies it:

> They that sow in tears shall reap in joy.
> Sorrow is better than laughter:
>> for by sadness of the countenance the heart is made better.
> Even in laughter the heart is sorrowful,
>> and the end of that air is heaviness.

The latter proverb, which is found in *Ecclesiastes*, took successive bows in the irony of Villon ("I laugh in tears"), Beaumarchais ("I laugh at everything for fear of being obliged to weep"), Byron ("And if I laugh at any mortal thing/'Tis that I may not weep") and the Mississippi bluesman Joe Callicott ("When you see me laughin' I'm laughin' just to keep from cryin'").

In the Middle Ages, when the Biblical view of earthly life as a vale of tears was probably most prevalent, studied melancholy became the characteristic mien of the nobleman. A historian remarks of this group: "There is hardly one who does not come forward to affirm that he has seen nothing but misery during his life and expects only worse things from the future."[1] Such maudlin affirmations often took the form of ballads (some of which were called "Lamentations") whose focus on love as both a balm against sorrow and the very bane of happiness fixed the perspective of all conventional love song to come. There is even a troubador love lyric that foreshadows a country blues couplet:

> *O God, were I a bird! I'd fain*
> *Across the earth take flight*
> *And ere the stars of night should wane*
> *By her would I alight.*

Translated into blues-speak on a recording by George Torey, the lyric is rendered:

> *If I had wings I'd fly like Noah's dove*
> *I'd hoist my wings and fly light on the woman I love.*

No less than heady romantic transports, melancholy long served as the opiate of countless insipid poets and a sentimental public Flaubert ridicules in his *Dictionary of Platitudes* with the comment that sorrow "always has beneficial consequences". Yet the idea that heartbreak could result in physical death may have also spurred its expression; as Macduff was counselled: "Give sorrow words: the grief that does not speak/Whispers the o'erfraught heart and bite it break." For whatever reasons, an astonishing assortment of English idioms (some dating to Elizabethan times) existed in the nineteenth century to literally give sorrow words: one spoke of the "blackdogs", the "blue devils", the "dismals", the "dumps", the "hyps", the "mopes", the "morbs", the "mulligrubs", the "mumps", the "wiffle-woffles", the "woefuls", the "worrits", and the "vapors". By contrast, there were few expressions conveying high spirits or describing a habitually dejected person.

As a figure of speech, the word "blues" (deriving from "blue devils") was bandied about quite casually in nineteenth century American conversation, or so an English novelist implied when he offered his readers this "speciman of Yankee dialect" in the 1830s: "I were thinking of Sal mysel, for I feel lonesome, and when I am thrown into my store promiscuous alone, I can tell you that I have the blues, the worst kind, no mistake—I can tell you that."[2] Presposing a journey with Hawthorne in 1851, Melville suggests: "But ere we start, we must dig a deep hole, and bury all Blue

1 Huizinga: *The Waning Of The Middle Ages*: Doubleday and Co.: New York: 1954: p. 34.
2 M.M. Mathews: *The Beginnings Of American English*: University of Chicago Press: Chicago: 1931: p. 135.

Devils, there to abide till the Last Day." When his wife bemoans slavery as a plague, the planter Augustine St. Claire of *Uncle Tom's Cabin* (1852) brushes aside her objection with the words: "O, come Marie, you've got the blues this morning."

The nonchalant and unselfconscious mention of "blues" in such contexts suggests that fits of dejection were taken for granted by our rugged forefathers, who are described in George R. Stewart's *American Ways of Life* as "serious to the point of being glum" and who impressed de Tocqueville with their "astonishing gravity" in the 1840s. Some sense of this bygone gloominess emerges in the nineteenth century hymn, with its presupposition that a secular existence leaves man in continual torment. It implores the unconverted, a "child of sorrow and woe", who is "weary laden, sick with heartache that earth cannot ease", or "o'erwhelmed with sorrow and care", or "bow'd and crush'd with years of sorrow", to seek solace in a Lord (the "Man of Sorrows" or the "Comforter") who provides "the hope of the desolate" and a cushion against "life's dark vale", "the night so still and long", "the land of endless day", "life's stormy pillows", "the strife of life", "the world's fruitless striving", and so on. Even the secular songs of the period were so downcast that Sigmund Spaeth remarks on the "misery fetish" of the nineteenth century American pop composer.

Had the black arrived in America as an equal rather than as chattel he would have doubtless acquired a similarly bleak *a priori* view of existence. With the Christianization of the slave he seems to have done so, although dour America (perhaps through its smug sense of superior desolation) continued to frown upon him as a carefree pagan. A forlorn Negro the journalist Olmsted encountered on a Mississippi road in the 1850s exclaimed: "Dis world ain't nothin'; dis is hell, dis is, I calls it; hell to what's a comin' arter, ha! ha!"[1]

Of itself the song conceit of "having the blues" attests to nothing else but this superficial Americanization—or Christianization—of the subjected black. The moroseness of Christian piety notwithstanding, nearly every country bluesman seems to understand his work as but an inversion of the spiritual, expressing the earthly cares or discontents that are supposed to be transcended in the glow of revival sentiment. With this logic he unwittingly embraces the very Fundamentalist doctrine that looked askance at blues for not directly partaking of religious ecstasy, for it was a church supposition that no one could happily abandon himself to any form of secular activity. (In the parlance of the black spiritual, the unredeemed was a "mourner".) Hence it is by no means unlikely that the designation of the black's basic secular music genre as "blues" was originally the figment of religious zealotry. On the other hand, it is no less plausible that folk osmosis of a sentimental stereotype of black music led to the christening of blues, the supposedly sad quality of such music having been practically the extent of nineteenth century observation upon it. Higginson found the spirituals he heard while commanding a black Civil War regiment in South Carolina "almost too sad to dwell upon", while Edward King was prepared to state a decade later, on the basis of what was surely a fleeting exposure to black music, that it was "the outgrowth of great and unavoidable sorrows, which force the heart to voice its cry. . ."[2] Considering the pity that the black's miserable estate in American life was liable to evoke in sympathetic outsiders, and the currency of the long outmoded doctrine of affections (which interpreted music in the light of a single underlying emotion), it is hardly surprising to come upon such explanations of Negro song. As for the bereaved Uncle Tom of *Massa's In De Cold Cold Ground* (1852) who tells us: *I try to drive away my sorrow; Pickin' on de old banjo*, he represents a campy Southern stereotype of a different sort. It may or may not have been prophetic that just seven

---

1 Olmsted: *The Cotton Kingdom*: Modern Library edition: New York: 1969: p. 364.
2 Higginson's *Army Life In A Black Regiment* (originally published in 1869) and King's *The Great South* (1875) were among the earliest works commending spirituals to the American public, although both treated the subject in passing.

years before the appearance of the first published blues the black poet Paul Dunbar would play upon the same image in a poem called *Blue*, whose grief-stricken narrator reaches for his banjo with the words: *"Tain't no use in talkin'/Chile, I's sholy blue."*

If even the spirituals that were supposed to smote sorrowful sentiment came to be labelled as "Sorrow Songs" by the turn of the century writer DuBois, a blues genre by any other name would have excited remarks upon its mournful character. For the critic and bluesman alike, the arbitrary use of the term "blues" to describe what had probably been a pre-existent song form[1] (by a process that is now only speculative) was no less than providential. It not only gave second wind to an exceedingly trite perception of black music (the popular notion still persists that blues are nothing more than a "worried mind") but provided the musician himself with a convenient framework in which to couch his rhymed ruminations. From a highly circumscribed catalogue of woes, the blues singer belabored the same motifs that were supposed to exemplify sorrow to the point of exhaustion. The most formulized blues confection deals not with sad sentiment per se, but with an event that occasions it, which may be anything from a mosquito bite to a poor telephone connection. Of the entire species of blues artist, the country bluesman (as distinct from the vaudeville or city speciman) probably has the least self-conscious and stylized approach. His songs are generally so episodic in nature that the occasion of his "blues" often remains unfocused: a Charlie Patton will evidently suffer the "overseas blues" or the "Green River blues" simply by virtue of setting foot upon such territory. When the country bluesman's song references to his own dejection are not gratuitous, as in the oft-used phrase "Got the blues, can't be satisfied", he tends to rationalize this feeling in terms of whiskey and women. With the same convention in mind, a country blues singer named Tom Nelson asked waggishly, on a 1928 recording: *I wonder why white folks don't have the blues? They drink plenty of whiskey, got brownskin women, too.*

By the time country bluesmen like Nelson were recorded in the late Twenties the aforementioned white misery fetish had indeed become something of a cultural relic, although a lower-class Middletowner grumbled to the Lynds that "sometimes the blues lasts a week." As everyone knows, the sober countenance of Puritanism was evaporated by Jazz Age euphoria, with its false promise of fulfillment through guileless hedonism and the pursuit of wealth.[2] But if a typical Twenties' gesture such as the public burial of "J. Fuller Gloom" by St. Augustine's Chamber of Commerce now seems quaint or ridiculous, so does the brooding of the country blues artist, if taken at face value. Even in this age of studied malaise, such depression is considered a matter for psychiatric referral, and there is no living idiom like "blues" to describe it. It is only by imagining the glib heartache of blues to be a unique racial product of social deprivation that the modern critic can basically forbear it. From such a perspective he can also exploit it, as Franz Fanon once observed:

> . . . the blues 'plaint of the Negro slaves' is offered to the admiration of the oppressors. It is a bit of stylized oppression which brings a profit to the exploiter and the racist. No oppression and no racism: no blues. The end of racism would sound the knell of the great Negro music.
>
> As the too celebrated Toynbee would say, the blues is the slave's response to the challenge of oppression.
>
> Even today for many people, including some coloured people, Negro music has no real meaning except in this perspective.[3]

---

1 Remarking on the musicians he heard as a youth, the late Reverend Gary Davis (1896–1972) once said: "People back in them times didn't know nothin' *about* what (kind of music) they played. They just played." Most of the early pieces he learned were untitled.

2 A blues development of the Twenties known as "hokum" and represented by such artists as Papa Charlie Jackson is quite faithful to the tenor of the Jazz Age.

3 Fanon: "Racism and Culture": *Streets Magazine*: New York: Vol. 1, No. 9: May-June 1965.

No matter what emotional motley the country bluesman chooses to wear or what sources he uses to arrive at his verse, his lyrics are basically a form of black utterance set to rhyme. As such they are unique: it goes without saying that they are a foreign tongue to the average white listener, whose only hope as a performer is to emulate it. Whether country blues dialect successfully resists adaptation by the now familiar white interpreter is a matter of aesthetic preference; within the bounds of this inquiry I shall content myself with the observation that it does not lend itself favorably to the printed page. Not even a phonetic transcription of country blues song could begin to convey the drawling inflections that permit the singer to arrive at false rhymes ("myself"/"else", "knee"/ "please", "back"/"like", "here"/"care") by emphasizing or bending assonant sounds[1], or the lush cadences that sweeten his most awkward sentences. Nor could the printed page do full justice to those country blues whose impact does not depend on such nuances of diction; there is an inevitable disparity between conversational and written expression, for which reason a play is said not to read as well as it performs. Finally, the immediate object of country blues verse is to move or mesmerize the listener, not to engage his dispassionate critical senses. Thus it frequently shares the logical bankruptcy of political oratory, not to mention that of an archetypal spellbinder, the old-fashioned black preacher. In its very lack of continuity, country blues invites comparison to Biblical expression, particularly that of *Psalms*.

Paradoxically, the determination to be realistic and to make sensible statement often proves the country bluesman's undoing, from an artificial literary standpoint. The country blues couplet is simply too terse to throw any real light on the dramas it characteristically portrays. Although the artist seems determined to disclose a life-like story, the curtain closes after revealing only the bare essentials of his dilemma. Only the listener who is already pre-disposed to accept the blues' facile fly-in-the-ointment formula can appreciate the lucidity of a song like Isaiah Nettles' *Mississippi Moan*:

> *Hey, somethin' going on wrong*
> *Know when I come in, find my baby gone.*
>
> *Oh, when she come in, rag tied on her head*
> *Asked my baby two questions, she swore she was nearly dead...*
>
> *Said I'm on my way back, to that lonesome hill*
> *'Cause that's where I can look down,*
> *   where this black man used to live.*
>
> *...I said mama what's gonna become of me?*
> *Every time I leave home, says I'm gonna follow that bumble bee.*
>
> *Lord, my bumble bee mama, caused me to leave my old home*
> *Lord, I tried and I tried, and I just can't let her alone.*

Here Nettles is struggling with two separate stories: a disintegrating love affair, jeopardized by the unreliability (or infidelity) of his mate, and his own vagabond lust, neither of which are explained to the satisfaction of a mildly curious listener. In his apparent preoccupation with the pet country blues notions that women and passion work insidious effects, and his determination to cast himself a victim of circumstances, Nettles ignores the wherefores of his situation. He fails to tell us why his woman absents herself from his household, what two test-questions she apparently flunks on her return, what conceivable solace can be derived from looking upon his old residence, why his "bumble bee" mama is able to distract him to the point of losing his mate, why he is unable to resolve the conflict by domesticating the "bumble bee" and ousting her rival.

As a rule, the country blues that bank on verisimilitude similarly beg ulterior questions and likewise suffer from superficiality. Perhaps the

---

Other false rhymes are attained through the devices of apocope ("do'"/"sow", "man"/"han'", "town"/"boun'") and syncope ("ho'n" for "horn" or "bo'n" for "born" to rhyme with "gone").

country bluesman whose couplets were best reconciled to the discursive format of the idiom was the great Blind Lemon Jefferson, whose superior talents as a versifier must have had some bearing on his singular commercial recording success in the Twenties. By striving for exotic and even surrealistic effects Jefferson neatly (if inadvertently) avoided the pitfall of spinning a half-told tale. To embellish Jefferson's off-beat efforts into full-blown themes would spoil them entirely:

> *Blues jumped a rabbit, run him one solid mile*
> *That rabbit fell down, cryin' like a natural child.*
>
> *I've got ten little puppies, I've got twelve little shaggy hounds*
> *Well it's gonna take them twenty-two dogs to run my kid gal down.*
>
> *I got up this mornin', ramblin' for my shoe*
> *The little woman sent me a saucerful of worried blues.*
>
> *I'm goin' to the river, gonna carry my rocker chair*
> *Gonna ask that tadpole soon*
>   *"Has the worried blues retched (reached) here?*

Whether by accident or design, country blues verse in its most familiar (and probably original) form is a non-sequential series of couplets, each one an entity in itself. Jumping capriciously from subject to subject, country blues seems diffuse by comparison to the Negro toast (a generally ribald first or third-person narrative which sometimes uses blues rhymes), the so-called minstrel song (a sixteen bar work roughly contemporary with country blues, comically depicting the escapades of a "bad nigger")[1], or the vaudeville blues popularized by the early Twenties recordings of band vocalists such as Bessie Smith or Ma Rainey. A non-thematic country blues, however, may present two serial couplets, or generally address itself to a given motif in the fashion of Sam Butler's *Poor Boy Blues*, a bald portrayal of hardship. Narrative development, continuity, or climax remains basically foreign to country blues, and is scarcely permitted by the bluesman's tendency to sing in the present tense or to concern himself with events of the immediate past.

Because of its hermetic quality a country blues verse shares the proverb's facility to breed counter propositions. Thus in the same song *Knocking Down Windows*, Mance Lipscomb variously informs the listener that a jet-black woman can "make a rabbit hug a hound" but "can't stay in my house lot", evidently fearing no contradiction in the process. On the other hand, it is simply poor plotting that leads Skip James to situate a thousand well-wishers at his bedside in *Sick Bed Blues* after having opened his song with the plaint: "I used to have a few friends but they wish that I was dead." Country bluesmen seemed to have marked difficulty in piecing together an episodic or narrative song, as Willie Walker's version of the traditional *Betty and Dupree* (a blues ballad based on a 1921 cop-killing in Atlanta) demonstrates. The first verse of Walker's song implies a motive for Dupree's crime: he wishes to gratify Betty's desire for a diamond ring. Having thus set the stage for a robbery, the song cuts straightaway to Dupree's murder of a policeman. Although he blames his predicament on Betty, he implores her to visit his cell in a follow-up verse. The song fades out on her request to see her "used-to-be", an expression that would indicate a falling-out had taken place between them.[2] In presenting songs with a chorus a country bluesman often begins with verses that are designed to set up a given catchphrase ("Snatch it and grab it", "Hang it on the wall"), only to fall back on successive reiterations of the chorus or

---

1 For an example of the "minstrel" song, see Frank Stokes' *I Got Mine*.
2 Some blues experts would ascribe such incongruities to the recording process itself on the grounds that a three minute recording limited blues to six or seven stanzas. While some songs were doubtlessly emasculated under these conditions, the inability (or disinclination) of the average artist to sustain themes or make original song statements suggests the opposite. It is of course easier to create six than sixty stanzas, and a witness of Willie Brown's live blues performances informs Gayle Wardlow that once that artist had delivered the verses that comprise his recording of *Future Blues* (q.v.) he would simply repeat them.

completely unrelated verses as inspiration flags.

Yet the usual scatter-gun style of country blues recitation is for the most part deliberate. The same seemingly random order of verses is likely to be preserved in alternate studio takes of the same song. Presented with a ready-mix blues recipe, the artist concocts a tossed salad. Charlie Patton's recorded adaptation of Shelley Bragg's *Bird Nest Blues* splinters the original theme beyond recognition. The "bird nest" of Bragg's song is a speakeasy:

> *Baby come and go, out to the edge of town*
> *I know where there's a place, there's a bird nest on the ground.*
>
> *Just as they played the music, all the music filled the air*
> *We thought we was in heaven, we found a bird nest there.*
>
> *When we would get lonesome, and everything was dull and calm*
> *Then we would get a taxi, and be bird nest bound.*
>
> *Just as they played Home Sweet Home,*
> * the men stepped up with shinin' star*
> *Say you don't need no taxi, I'll take you in my car.*
>
> *If I was a bird I'd build my nest in the heart of town*
> *Oh lord, just as sure as in the air*
> *So when the police raid it, wouldn't find it on the ground nowhere.*

By recapitulating the opening verse and making a composite of the third and final couplets, Patton remodels the bird nest into a lover's rendezvous. He proceeds to fly the coop with three successive verses relating to no subject in particular. This accomplished, he fouls the nest altogether by concluding with a bizarre paraphrase of Bragg's fourth verse: *Safe sweet home now, through that shinin' star; You don't need no tellin' mama I will, take you in my car.* Two verses of Patton's *Bird Nest Bound* subsequently came to roost on his recording of *Revenue Man Blues*, where they mark a departure from an opening theme sustained for two verses. To Patton's one-time associate Son House such digressions compromised him as a versifier. Actually, they are fundamental to country blues, whose basic underpinnings do not rest with the juxtaposition of its verses but with the internal agreement of its individual couplets.

The impact of the individual couplet derives from a kind of strophe and antistrophe, with the answering half of the verse serving to illuminate an initial statement that is so constructed as to beg for completion.[1] A self-conscious composer may deliberately heighten anticipation of his disclosing phrase with a provocative or enigmatic set-up line. To Skip James, an opener like "I would rather be buried, in some cypress grove" was basically a riddle designed to spark an imaginary dialogue between himself and the listener: "Say, 'Why'd you rather be buried in a cypress grove, Skip?' I say: 'I'd rather be buried there than to have a contentious woman, or one that I can't control.'"

The most artless form of blues verse (save that which does not rhyme at all) stitches together two unrelated statements on the slender thread of rhyme:

> *Hey Lord have mercy, on my wicked soul*
> *I wouldn't mistreat you baby, for my weight in gold.*
> *Jackson on a high hill mama, Natchez just below*
> *I ever get back home I, won't be back no more.*

But no matter how well country blues phrases appear to mesh they exist by virtue of their rhyming facility.[2] To a large degree in country blues, rhyme occurs sheerly for its own sake and crowds out such considerations as subject matter. As Skip James once described the art of blues composition:

> . . . You could make a song or verse out of most any common ordinary

---

1 Although the conventional blues stanza actually consists of three lines, the invariable repetition of the first makes it essentially a couplet.
2 Only two known bluesmen deliberately sing blank verse: Booker White and Robert Pete Williams.

thing: 'Bad, bad whiskey.' You could say . . . that 'Whiskey caused me to go astray, to lose my happy home . . . So I decided to leave that whiskey alone, till I get so I can go back home.' That's a rhyme, right there . . . Now then, you could rhyme a song in this way, say: 'My baby has left me; I can see her 'cross the river to the other side. And when she left me, she left me a mule to ride.' See that? That rhymes in and compares with the first phrase that you made . . .

The perfection of the rhyme is probably less important than the "comparison" it forms with its antecedent. But by the same token the country bluesman is scrupulous enough about preserving the facade of rhyme to obliterate sounds that prevent him from attaining it; he will even mute the fricative consonant in "blues" in order to facilitate a rhyme with a word like "too" or "do".

Despite its guileless reaching for rhyme, country blues comes equipped with so many stock rhyme words (say/away; time/mind; me/be) that a given couplet normally manages to take its bow without visible strain. In its simple couplet rhyming pattern, its haste to arrive at a grammatically complete statement, and its basic subservience to rhyme itself, the country blues resembles nothing so much as the nursery rhyme. Given this stylistic resemblance and the discernable white parallels between folk song and Mother Goose it is tempting to theorize country blues origins in black nursery rhymes. A Fisk professor once observed: "Many Negro Folk Rhymes were used as banjo and fiddle (violin) songs . . . these were quite often repeated without singing or playing. It was common in the early days of the public schools of the South to hear Negro children use them as declamations."[1] Unfortunately, no rhymes from this period that might have later seen duty as country blues verses appear to be extant. The only discoverable nursery rhyme precedents for blues verses are Anglo-Saxon, such as a nineteenth century jingle taken up by Charlie Pickett and Mance Lipscomb: "My little old man and I fell out; I'll tell you what 'twas all about . . ."

The country blues gimmick of entwining two completely alien phrases, the first a nonsensical teaser, is a familiar nursery rhyme convention. Blind Lemon Jefferson was particularly partial to this verse format:

No more potatoes, this frost has killed the vine
Well the blues ain't nothin' but a good woman on your mind.

So cold in China, the birds can't hardly sing
You didn't make me mad, till you broke my diamond ring.

So many wagons, they done tore the Good Road down
And the gal I love, her mama don't want me around.

Oh, lordie how the sun do shine
And I can't get the job done, with that brownskin gal of mine.

A few Charlie Patton blues endeavors smack of white nursery rhyme:

Sometimes I say I need you, then again I don't
Sometimes I think I'll quit you, then again I won't.

I know my dog anywhere I hear him bark
I can tell my rider if I feel her in the dark.

One imagines the artist's boyhood ears pricking up at the savage jungle cries:

He loves me, he don't
He'll have me, he won't.

Home went the little woman all in the dark
Up starts the little dog and he began to bark.[2]

However curious, the coincidence between a country blues and nursery rhyme couplet is less indicative of any historical link between the two forms than of their mutual diffusiveness. Both the country blues and nursery

---

1 Thomas W. Talley: *Negro Folk Rhymes, Wise and Otherwise*: Macmillan: New York: 1922: p. 235.

2 Nocturnal recognition is also the subject of this couplet, which the *Oxford Dictionary Of Nursery Rhymes* dates to the eighteenth century.

rhyme couplet exist as such only by usage and circumstance. The fact that there is no such thing as a country blues couplet by definition not only gives the performer license to create but license to borrow whatever material he cares to palm off as blues. His underlying sources may be as remote from his immediate environment as the genteelism of Burns' *A Red Red Rose* taken up by Ishman Bracey and Skip James: "And I will luve thee still, my dear/ Till a' the seas gang [*gone*] dry." As one might expect, the traditional spiritual provided rich fare for country blues paraphrase, some of it deliberately sacrilegious:

> *It was early one mornin' just 'bout the break of day*
> *When my long brownskin come in here and throwed me 'way.*
>
> *What make I love my baby so?*
> *She makes five dollars and she give me four.*

With these affirmations the country bluesmen Garfield Akers and Willie Harris may be laughing at the expense of the antebellum spiritual:

> *. . . It was early in the morning*
> *Just at the break of day*
> *When he rose, when he rose, when he rose.*
>
> *What makes old Satan hate me so?*
> *He had me once and let me go.*

But most of all country blues verse feeds on itself. Equally amenable to plagiary and paraphrase, it also lends itself favorably to subdivision. Mississippi bluesmen, for example, have a variety of retorts to the root statement "I went to the depot, I looked upon the board":

> *Well I couldn't see no train I couldn't hear no whistle blow.*
> *If this train has left well it's tearin' off up the road.*
> *Said: "If your baby ain't here she'll be, long ways up the road."*
> *I asked the conductor: "How long,*
> *   has this eastbound train been gone?"*

In addition to its wealth of portable or collapsible couplets, and its various stock masculine rhymes, country blues has a modest portfolio of catchwords and catchphrases all of its own. Some of them are idiomatic expressions that probably attained song currency through their potential scanning or rhyming value; others are merely decorative. The country bluesman has a certain fondness for bridging two adjectives or verbs with the conjunction "and"[1]; he indulges this mannerism with some of his characteristic song phrases. A stubby woman is invariably "low and squatty"; her physical opposite, "long and tall", or simply "long-tall". With similar redundancy he speaks of the dead as "dead and gone", a perverse coupling since nineteenth century euphemism politely referred to the dead as "gone before". If the bluesman is convinced that his termination of a love affair will prove as irrevocable as death, or will produce funereal gloom in the rejected lover, he tells her: "I'm gonna hang crepe on your door." Using dated synecdoche, he designates a household with the expression "door"; if his own door is closed to him, he is "driven" from this door or finds his trunk set outdoors. Amicable parting mandates a "fare thee well", the archaic equivalent of "Good luck, kid." Histrionics inevitably accompany blues tears: the stricken suitor must "weep and moan", or wring his hands and cry. In the country blues lexicon it is too imprecise to mention a morning, and let it go at that; the modifications "early this morning" or "soon this morning" are preferable. If prior events did not transpire "late last night", they are not worth mentioning, unless they occurred "'fore day" (before daybreak). Human hair that is not coal-black is unworthy of color, although human complexion may appear jet-black. If the sea is to have any physical properties, it must be deep and blue; it is always best glimpsed from a mountain top. The landlubber does not light out for the woods; he

---

1 E.g., "young and wild", "low and lonesome", "sick and bad", "bred and born", "kind and sweet", "down and out", "worried and bothered", "screamed and squalled".

heads "up the country". In country bluesdom all roads lead not to Rome but to Alabama, a generic nineteenth century expression for the South that the artist seems to use neither figuratively nor literally, but superfluously. Perhaps the sociologically-oriented blues critic can explain the meaning of this great exodus:

> *The Kate's in the bed; the Stack is turnin' 'round and round*
> *The sternwheel knockin', I'm Alabama bound.*
>
> *The dicks told Casey: "You must leave town"*
> *"I believe to my soul I'm Alabama bound."*
>
> *I looked to the east, and I looked to the west*
> *If she headed for the South, she's Alabama bound.*
>
> *Here comes Number Three, with her headlights on top*
> *I believe to my soul, she's Alabama bound.*

Were country blues a self-conscious poetic exercise, such phrase-mongering would discredit his undertaking. However, the bluesman's interests lie not so much in the direction of verbal gymnastics as in the physical variety. It is action that sets the tone of most country blues verses, and phrases like "Alabama bound" are merely employed to this end. Motion is the single property that sufficiently intrigues the artist to bring out the original wordsmith in him. The colorful and sensuous verbal expressions by which he animates persons, objects, and even sentiments form his chief contribution to American speech. His words gyrate no less than his music. A country bluesman is not just distracted; he finds his mind "ramblin'". He does not party; he "barrelhouses". He does not work, but "rolls". His trains come "easin'" or "rollin'" by, and the artist's own activity is given the same supple quality. King Solomon Hill intends to "ease it back to Tennessee"; Garfield Akers pictures himself "rollin' out" of a stopped train; Willie Newbern "rolls and tumbles" in agitation. Charlie Patton "tips" around town in search of quickie sex. The blues "creep up" on Ishman Bracey and Joe Callicott; Son House sees them "walkin' just like a man". Blind Boy Fuller's professed love is so staunch "it can't be turned around". Blind Willie McTell sings the praises of the "Statesboro darkskin" who will "really turn your damper down"; the jet-black woman, Son House advises us, will "make a mule kick his stable down". Robert Johnson's woman has "Elgin movements" and "breaks in on a dollar"; Blind Blake's audience flocks to Wabash Avenue to "break 'em down" (frolic). Furry Lewis threatens to "shake 'em on down" (bug out) when a would-be lover appears stand-offish; Mance Lipscomb goes "knockin' down windows and tearin' around doors" after a romantic betrayal. A country bluesman is "thrown down" (or away) by a fickle mistress, and "dogged around" by a clinging vine. Willie Baker wags a finger at the gullible woman whose paramours "tear her down"; Joe McCoy, enjoying the affections of such a dupe, proudly proclaims: "She tore up my trouble, broke up my misery."

Because the action country blues depicts is predominately realistic, the distinction between figurative and literal phrases it employs is readily blurred, particularly when such phrases hinge upon nouns. One cannot distinguish whether the hellhound that pursues Robert Johnson is meant to be an actual creature or a metaphor for religious transgression. Either a bulldog or a pistol (commonly known as a "bulldog" in slang usage) may be invoked by Blind Joe Reynolds' phrase: "I'm gonna buy me a bulldog, watch my old lady whilst I sleep." When Sam Collins sings: "I was layin' in jail with my back turned to the wall" he may be either assuming a physical posture or using a standard idiom for calamity. When Charlie Patton turns his face to the wall as a "jinx" descends upon him he may be simply facing a wall, or miming the proverbial repose of the dying. By holding her head high, bluesdom's familiar "crow jane" may be bowing to the cliché figure of nineteenth century speech expressing haughtiness or impudence, or doing nothing of the kind. For couplets of this kind have a built-in ambiguity; their circulation among different artists was probably a measure of the musicians' lack of introspection. Once a song expression became part of the country blues lexicon, it acquired a life of its own, sometimes losing meaning in the process. To Leadbelly the blues catchphrase "careless love" implied unrequited love, in which one party did not "care" for the other. The famous song of the same name was a ballad of remorse. But the original "Careless Love", the protagonist of Ravenscroft's drama *Careless Lovers* (1673), personified carefree love (or what we would now understand as free love), an activity he championed as "more cheerful" than monogamy. One suspects similar erosion in the meaning of song phrases like "salty dog" or "crow jane", which struck at least one bluesman as forming animal comparisons, although they are unquestionably figurative.

While country blues has its moments of cant it is never so nonsensical as one would have been led to believe by the academic stereotypes of black folk song as being "generally defective in prosody and without merit, being often little more than words strung together to carry an air", to cite an 1890 encyclopedia appraisal. That the texts of black folk songs were not only dismissed in this fashion but were rarely analyzed even by those who bothered to collect them during the Twenties is partly attributable to the white view of the Negro mentality as a dark void masking itself with a "racial relish for impressive words and resounding sentences".[1] As the folklorist Puckett wrote in 1926: "The Negro is constantly being lost in a labyrinth of jaw-breaking words full of sound and fury but signifying nothing."[2] Cash's highly regarded study of the South included the observation:

> . . . nothing is so certain as his [the Negro's] remarkable tendency to seize upon lovely words, to roll them in his throat, to heap them in redundant profusion one upon another until meaning vanishes and there is nothing left but the sweet, canorous drunkenness of sound, nothing but the play of primitive rhythm upon the secret springs of emotion.[3]

Given an Anglo-Saxon relish for platitudes it was inevitable that a compiler of black folk song (writing in 1928) should assert the singer's "invincible racial indifference to the meaning of words and verbal structure in songs."[4] It was no less inevitable that the same imagined trait would give black utterance, from an avant-garde literary viewpoint, the pregnancy of a Molly Bloom soliloquy. The protaganist of Sherwood Anderson's *Dark Laughter* (1925) is moved by black singing to reflect: "The word, as meaning, of no importance. Perhaps words were always unimportant." When Gertrude Stein showcased the technique of automatic writing (in which words had no meaning except as vocables) her producers chose a black cast to recite the lines of *Four Saints In Three Acts* (1934) on the premise that nonsensical expression would be second nature for it.

The reputation of the black speaker or singer for making imbecilic statements may have been the legacy of antebellum minstrel song, which used incoherence for comic effect in its boorish portrayal of the plantation slave. Perhaps the notion that blacks had a peculiar fondness for high-flown verbiage was formed by taking in the rhetoric of the black pastor, although he was far less fabled for this idiosyncrasy than the Western frontiersman. A scrutiny of country blues produces an altogether different impression of black speech, at least as it existed in the rural South during the Twenties. Considering the fact that the blues medium was conceived to entertain, its overall lucidity is quite astonishing. Only a few country blues *(Keep It Clean, Mamlish Blues)* make a willing surrender to gibberish, and these do so facetiously. Far from being grandiloquent, the style of blues expression is so matter-of-fact and prosaic as to make the English ballads whose language was often acclaimed for its "simplicity" and "lack of adornment" seem ornate by comparison. The tone of country blues is un-

1 Clifton Johnson: *Highways and Byways Of The South*: Macmillan Company: New York: 1904: p. 334.
2 Newbell Niles Puckett: *Folk Beliefs Of The Southern Negro*: Dover reprint: New York: p. 28.
3 W.J. Cash: *The Mind Of The South*: Vintage reprint of the 1941 edition: New York: 1960: p. 53.
4 Cf. White: p. 4. His own indifference asserted itself when he treated "Rackensack" (an archaic expression for Arkansas) as a song mispronunciation of "Hackensack".

mistakably conversational; its metaphors and similes distinctly colloquial. As would be customary of everyday speech, it bothers with few adjectives. The recurrent modifiers in the country blues lexicon are "poor", "lowdown", "lonesome", and "worried", applied to persons, places, or states of feeling.[1] The nouns country blues employs are nearly always concrete; besides the "blues" that creep, walk, and jump rabbits, immaterial or invisible entities do not exist for the artist.

Despite its pithiness, the country blues idiom is flecked with such superfluous and probably unconscious conversational mannerisms as the habit of prefacing statements with "Says" or "I says", a locution that needlessly converts them into direct dialogue. Characteristically, blues verse is launched with some preliminary expectoration that conveys a sense of the singer's breathing presence but appears distracting in print: "Well . . .", "You know . . .", "Lookey here . . .", "It's . . .", or "An' . . ."[2]. Such quirks of diction are probably most pronounced in the delivery of Mississippi bluesmen like Charlie Patton or Son House. It is probably no coincidence that over a third of the black Mississippians born between 1890-1900 (the general time span that witnessed the birth of most country bluesmen) were judged illiterate by the 1910 census.[3]

The intrinsic conversational quality of even the most articulate country blues can be related to its illiterate origins. Unlike any comparably unsophisticated group that produced music in America, the rural black was programmed to remain a folk people in a society that boasted a literacy rate of 90% at the turn of the century. Esteeming blacks in proportion to their docility and usefulness in labor, the Southern ruling classes traditionally equated Negro education with *uppityness*. Public money spent on so dubious a cause, argued governor Vardaman of Mississippi, could only serve to "spoil a good field hand and make an insolent cook." Throughout the Jim Crow era the length of the rural black school term was mediated by the growing season. An emphasis on the black's capacity as a worker at the expense of his intellectual advancement was also basic to the outlook of Booker T. Washington, who declared in his famous Atlanta Exposition speech that "No race can prosper till it learns that there is as much dignity in tilling a field as in writing a poem."

The backwardness of the language used by the country bluesman of the Twenties testifies to the brutal success of the endeavor to leave the rural black at the mercy of mother wit alone. In addition to its broken and frequently archaic syntax[4], country blues gives play to a variety of downtrodden superstitions, such as perceiving behaviour or character in terms of complexion: *Some crave high yellow, I like black or brown: Black won't quit you, brown won't lay you down.* Negro folk beliefs to the effect that sunshine always breaks through rainstorms, that the content of dreams has prognosticative value, and that the act of turning three times brings forth luck contribute to the zest of the blues phrases:

Let it rain today, sunshine in your—sunshine in your—I mean door
Did you ever dream lucky, wake up cold in hand?
She turned around, two-three times; begged my babe:
   "Take me back."

If the folklorist delighted in any appearance of black rusticity, the cultural lag between the rural black and mainstream America was the despair of those who wished to improve his social condition. Outside of rural blacks themselves and the white Southerners who accepted the idea of their innate musicality, few persons of either race had any kind of relish for the

1 "Poor boy", the country bluesman's favorite self-description, signifies misfortune, not poverty.
2 Sentences beginning with "And" are a stylistic convention of the Bible; they predominate in such blues as *Roll and Tumble*.
3 By contrast, only a fifth of the Texans polled in the same census were classified as illiterate. In general Texas blues display better verbal ability than their Mississippi counterparts.
4 Some apparently slipshod blues constructions, like the substitution of a personal for reflexive pronoun ("I'm gonna buy me a bulldog"), or the use of "were" instead of "was", are actually archaisms.

social type the country bluesman embodied. He received none of the popular appreciation accorded to jazz in the Twenties, when he was already culturally dated. The black folk sage had been nationally revered during the nineteenth century vogue for what was called "by gosh" literature; at the onset of country blues recording in the mid-Twenties the chief glories of the black race were thought to reside in the "new Negro". Nearly a quarter of a century before the *Times* had commended the "old-time darky" of the Mississippi Delta to its readers, a Southern educator had flatly proclaimed: ". . . the old-time darky is forever gone. He was the product of conditions of slavery . . . There are just two classes of negroes in our land to-day, those who are going forward and those who are going backward."[1] Even Faulkner, who had once drawn an unflattering fictional portrait of a black farmer idly peering at a volume through rimless glasses as his crops languished, would eventually pronounce the black who found his chief solace in such diversions as listening to his own music as the "second-rate" of his race.

Long before the northern city had siphoned off the bulk of the black farm population, the country blues had become the casualty of increased sophistication (or the desire for it) on the part of its "down home" audience. The black urbanite was statistically atypical in 1940, but the urban blues singer then enjoyed a total stranglehold on the blues recording market, which had opened up in 1920. The country bluesman had such a short life as a recording attraction that he may have already been aesthetically obsolete when he rode to the recording studio on the coat-tails of Blind Lemon Jefferson's wildly successful commercial debut of 1926. The original wave of blues recording had popularized a succession of vaudeville singers whose stock in trade was a chic image to which the country bluesman furnished no competition. Although the blues record consumer of the Twenties did not think in categories like "city" and "country" bluesman, he evinced a clear preference for the smooth performer who was able to render lyrics in clear diction or concoct full-dress song themes. This aesthetic augered against most country bluesmen, while rewarding their city counterparts like Lonnie Johnson, Leroy Carr, and Tampa Red. By the 1930s many of the previous decade's country bluesmen had begun to ape a city format. No one knows quite when country blues lost its neighborhood appeal, but the country bluesman born after the onset of World War One was a freak of nature. His undertaking had scant place in community ideals when Charles S. Johnson polled Black Belt students on the subject of career preferences in the mid-Thirties. Fewer than three per cent of the males who responded aspired to a profession in music; nearly five times their number wished to become schoolteachers.

Today's armchair blues listener is scarcely able to appreciate the negative image that blues of even the most sophisticated stripe presented to the success-oriented black of the Twenties. Nor, perhaps, could the country bluesman himself comprehend the middle-class rejection of his music with the detached class perspective of a Pete Franklin, who still perpetuates the all but dead blues traditions of his native Indianapolis. "Here's what makes me shitty," the 45-year old Franklin complains. "The middle-class colored man's the man that looked down on blues: he taught his kids to look down on it because it associated him back to slavery. . . He wanted to forget about that shit; he wanted his kids to forget that shit . . . He kept everybody else from appreciatin' it." In Franklin's view the blues presented the black *arriviste* with unpleasant reminders of his own scruffy social origins. Yet a certain prudence as well as an outright priggery may have figured in the middle-class black's sour reception of blues. However innocently, the subject matter of blues often manages to flatter some of the most detested stereotypes that shackled blacks during the Jim Crow period, a point that is somehow neglected by those who would make sociological hay of blues verse. The womanizing, drinking, gambling, and gold-bricking that pre-

1 Edward Gardner Murphy: *Problems Of The Present South*: Longmans, Green and Company reprint of the 1904 edition: New York: 1916, pp. 85–86.

empt countless blues couplets were the cardinal "vices" for which blacks were supposed to have a special aptitude.

For the country bluesmen these motifs were part of a religious rather than racial dialectic: in trading upon them they annointed themselves as devil's emissaries in the eyes of the church-goers who were already prepared to score any secular form of musical expression. Despite the self-proclaimed hedonism of so many blues lyrics, country bluesmen for the most part seem to have enacted their musical morality play with a good deal of squeamishness. They were remarkably susceptible to periodic displays of religious penitence; in some instances (one thinks of Robert Wilkins and Ishman Bracey) the conversion held good and foreclosed a musical career altogether. Although a country bluesman of the old school will convey the song impression that he is beleagured only by demonic women, or demon rum, and the critic of the new school will blame his disquietude upon adverse social conditions, the real hellhound on his trail (if there ever was one) was a pompous pastor. It was a rare country bluesman who could muzzle the beast with Pete Franklin's self-assured flippance: "That son of a bitch come tellin' me that's the works of the devil. I looked at him and said: 'How you figure it's (i.e., blues) the works of the devil? It ain't nothin' but some damn *music!*'

"He said: 'It suggests *sins.*'"

"I said: 'Suggests my ass, man! If a son of a bitch is gonna do somethin' he's gonna *do* it—he don't need *me* to play for him first, you dig what I mean?'"

But even the street-wise Franklin could feel an occasional twinge of religious ambivalence: confined to jail, he could not bring himself to use the pages of a Gideon Bible as cigarette paper. His country cousins were adverse to performing during a rainstorm, lest God smote them with thunderbolts. The country bluesman's capitulation to Fundamentalist rhetoric expresses itself in the self-lacerating attitudes of many of his verses. To explain his reversals he sometimes cites the Biblical saw that "whatsoever a man soweth, that shall he also reap," which had a counterpart in the Negro folk saying that "Trouble follows sin as sure as fever follows chills" and in the white proverb: "The devil's children have the devil's luck." He accepts the Puritan premise that his melodramatic downfall is of his own making:

What my mama told me, long done come to pass:
"Whiskey and women, poor boy'll be your ruin at last."

Oh, I'd a-had religion, lord this very day
But the womens and whiskey well they, would not set me free.

It was not the hard knocks of life, but the jaded wisdom of the proverb that effected this epiphany: two thousand years before it forcibly struck Sam Butler and Son House, an aphorist stated: "Wine and women will make men of understanding to fall away."

When the country bluesman appears to be vindicating himself by needling his favorite scapegoat—the preacher—he is neither making a target of a racial elite nor questioning the ideals the preacher ostensibly represents. Ordinarily, the rural black preacher was a farmer who adopted his vocation via the same "call" that gave the early American Baptist his theological credentials. Anyone so "called" could be a preacher, and anyone, it seemed, could dispute his authority. The bluesman does not sing from his special perspective when he stakes out his claim against preachers: his jibes fall somewhere amidst a confluence of Southern white, rural black, and middle-class black stereotypes that not only found their way into blues but into folk tales and even spirituals as well. The depiction of the preacher as a blackguard was basic to the medieval religious sensibility that plantation religious doings so often resembled. An English proverb published by George Herbert in 1649 declared: "The frier preached against stealing, and had a goose in his sleave." Some three hundred years later the same statement came to light as a black proverb collected in Vicksburg, Mississippi: "When dat preacher leaves my house I steps out in de backyard an' counts my chickens." The most popular blues put-down of the preacher conveys the same thought: *Some folks say that a preacher won't steal I caught two in my corn-field.* Scarcely a white chronicle was written about black society before the 1920s that did not include either a personal or general denunciation of black clergymen along similar lines. In part these attacks supported the popular suppositions that blacks were intrinsically pagan and that any route removing them from the cottonfield was necessarily a devious one. Far from defending such preachers from widespread charges of immorality, turn of the century black spokesmen gave credence to them. Recalling the days of Reconstruction, Booker T. Washington noted how "immoral men . . . claimed they were 'called to preach' in order to dodge the horrors of manual labor,"[1] a notion Son House advances in his 1930 recording of *Preachin' The Blues*:

> *Oh I'm gonna get me a religion, I'm gonna join the Baptist church*
> *I'm gonna be a Baptist preacher and I sure won't have to work.*

In a serious sociological study[2], DuBois once polled two hundred blacks in order to determine whether black preachers were "notoriously immoral", and accepted their subjective opinions at face value.[3] The Atlanta clergy to whom he personally gave high marks for upright conduct were themselves dismissed by a journalist (Ray Stannard Baker) a few years afterwards as "often the worst sort of characters, dishonest and immoral." In an era when even the black preacher seemed so disreputable, it is a small wonder that the country blues artist would remain persona non grata to the black middle class.

The bluesman better demonstrates his individual imagination in his ability to crystallize less promiscuous stereotypes of his own society in the form of blues verse. Although he seems predisposed to treat social types (as titles like *Weak-Minded Woman* or *Memphis Rounder's Blues* attest) our present paucity of information about rural black culture of the nineteenth and early twentieth century largely obscures them from our view. Nevertheless, folk corollaries exist to such creatures as the "kind-hearted woman" of Robert Johnson's song[4] and the lady who shams illness to avoid working for Ed Bell in *Hambone Blues*:

> *You come home, at night; she got a towel on her head*
> *Don't you mention about "rollin'" 'cause*
>   *she'll, swear she's nearly dead.*

Mississippi bluesman Booker White observes:

> . . . Some older women; they marry; they don't wanna work theirself; they wanna play 'pretty mama' and they want Roscoe to do the work, and they sit at the house; when he go to work, they hit the street lookin' for wine, whiskey, and stuff. And when he get off his job, some of 'em don't even be able to have the dinner done: they have a rag tied around their head, and they're the sickest thing in the hospital. But you see the husband don't know: she just been *drunk* all day.
>
> Now the reason Booker can talk that so good: I used to be with that bunch . . . I'd say: "Look: ain't y'all gonna cook your husbands nothin'?"
>
> They say: "I just ain't able, Booker; I'm tellin' you the truth. I'm gonna put a rag around my head and tell him I'm sick when he gets home." And she just fall over in the bed there with that rag; when he come in she be drunk . . .
>
> "Honey, what's the matter with *you*?"

1 *Up From Slavery*: Doubleday reprint of the 1902 edition: Garden City, New York: 1963: p. 58.
2 *The Negro Church*: Atlanta University Press: Atlanta: 1903.
3 I am unable to resist reporting the findings of a mathematical wizard from Coffeeville, Mississippi who disclosed that ten per cent of the preachers in his vicinity were immoral; two per cent, sexually impure; two per cent, dishonest in money matters; and six per cent, drunkards.
4 Piecing together the reminiscence of Skip James and Big Bill Broonzy in *Big Bill Blues*, she asserts herself by supporting a gigolo and exacting his fidelity at the risk of death.

"Aw, I take sick a while ago, and a pain hit me in my head."

Well, quite naturally, then, he gonna feel her pity, he say: "Well just lay on down then, I'll fix me somethin' . . ."

Such chronicles of the misdoings of the opposite sex consume a good deal of the country bluesman's creative energies, so much so that Skip James considered them the *raison d'être* of the blues form: ". . . It gives a person ideas about women; when they are contentious . . . I'll tell you, it's a lot of people have experienced those things about women. They've did all they could for 'em. And still they (the women) didn't appreciate it; give 'em no consideration . . . See, those kinda ideas I catch and I just convert 'em into music; songs, where they'll fit, an' heap of people hear those songs and know exactly—it hit *somebody*—I don't care what song you sing, it's gonna hit somebody; they're gonna talk about it."

Where feminism dictates the conversation, "talk" about country blues is likely to be disparaging. The Victorian long ago anticipated one obvious feminist objection to country blues: its lack of "higher sentiment" for the opposite sex scandalized the folklorist of the Twenties. Moreover, observers from Thomas Jefferson to W.E.B. DuBois felt that black men generally lacked the proper degree of romantic solicitude, and were not protective, patronizing, or prudish enough to make exemplary lovers and husbands. The country bluesman Jim Jackson couches a similar stereotype of the black male in the form of a blues proverb:

> Well a white man give his wife a ten dollar bill,
>   he thinks that's nothing strange
> But a colored man give his wife a one dollar bill,
>   and beat her to death about the ninety cents change.

In the country blues scheme it is more often the duplicity of the woman who pockets his change that calls for the singer's adverse comment. The wonder of all this is that he banked on his own in-person appeal to a female audience, while remorselessly flagellating it in song. If anything, he was less popular with the sex whose cause he adamantly represents.

As S.I. Hayakawa has previously noted, blues broods far less upon the far-fetched ideals of abstract love that puff up the pop song (and modern soul music) than upon tangible love relationships. In so doing, however, it is not necessarily any more realistic than pop music; the blues preoccupation with the forlorn results of its love affairs is nothing if not preordained. Its rhetorical terms for women can be equally artificial, ranging from the impertinence of "rider" (which one informant defines as meaning "a fuck") to the genteel formality of "fair brownie" (which combines the stock ballad equivalent for "pretty" with the once-fashionable term for an elf). In the same crazy quilt fashion, a country blues song can admit the most conventionally romantic sentiments alongside a denunciation of women so total as to make the modern listener shudder at its misogyny, unless he has the eunuch's envy for any masculine show of strength. The bluesman can oscillate between such poles because his perspective is neither romantic nor anti-romantic, but pre-romantic. Perhaps he did not so much reject the purple prose of the torch song as he was bewildered by it, in the manner of Pete Franklin: "You take, I call it sentimental music . . . I like a lot of it, but as far as gettin' a *feelin'* out of it, there's not a damn feelin' in it. Just some son of a bitch talkin' about the trees and the birds, and all that motherfuckin' bullshit. 'The cottage for sale' and all that . . . I love *I Surrender Dear*, but it's just 'cause I like the tone; I like the chords and so on. But the words: half of 'em don't even make sense. 'Lending a spice to the wooing'! —Gosh! What the fuck does that mean, do you know?"

It remains curious that the country bluesman of the Twenties managed to withstand the mooniness of the very love songs he sometimes performed for white audiences while remaining conventionally sentimental towards his mother and his dead mistresses, both of whom he martyrizes in song. His completely unceremonious approach to love comes closer to a rough composite of west African mores, which conducted marriage as a business proposition; Old Testament testimony, which divines deceit in fair words, particularly those of women, and old Anglo-Saxon adages: "The best of friends must part"; "You never miss your water till the well runs dry". To this background he brings his own sense of one-upmanship, basking in his superiority over the "monkey man" who indiscriminately welcomes the affections of the opposite sex, even when they are offered insincerely.

In complaining of the infidelity and insubordination of his own women, the country bluesman sets himself off from negative stereotypes like the monkey man. But while he appears no less interested in the problem of controlling women as his white boss was once obsessed with the techniques of "handling niggers", it is the breakdown of control or stability that his verses usually commemorate. The listener who hopes to use his material as "equipment for living" (its sublime function in Hayakawa's view) is thus left in total turmoil. The old Irish saying that "There are three things without rule: a mule, a pig, and a woman" is embodied not only in countless blues depictions of affairs gone to ruin through female treachery but in Blind Lemon Jefferson's own blues proverb:

The blues come to Texas, lopin' like a mule
You take a high-brown woman, man she's hard to rule.

To the "primitive" country bluesman money and lust appear to rule the affections, and he makes no exception of himself. Although he is always inclined to talk up his own sexual prowess he usually resents the romantic purchasing power of the dollar and derides the man who uses it to that end as a "fatmouth". He has numerous song equivalents to the proverbial view that "When poverty comes in at doors, love leaps out at windows" and that "Misfortune is friendless". Another old saw, "Trust your friends with that you need fear him if he were your enemy", probably underlies Robert Johnson's counsel to: "Watch your close friend baby, then your enemy can't do you no harm." When the enemy wears a dress the country bluesman is sometimes prepared to dispatch her with a barrage of blows or bullets; murder of retribution is generally acquitted by the blues jury. Love rivals are likewise given no quarter. Perhaps the most polemical country blues killing is the death of "crow jane" at the hands of Skip James, which is intended as an object lesson in mortality, the victim having ignored the popular nineteenth century aphorism, "You got to die someday", to which the bluesman subscribes with a medieval passion.[1] Such insight may be the reason why the blues bloodletting is never given the tragic dimension of the traditional murder ballad.

The blues outlook on women is colored not only by proverbial declaration but by the singer's own role-playing. He expresses the standpoint of the unmarried male and uses the vocabulary of the barrelhouser who patronized his own performances. Wives are given far less scrutiny than the blues party-girl, who is always fair game for opprobrium or verbal wolf-whistling. Much country blues commentary on love, sex, and sweet mama falls under the category of "woofing", a favorite party-goer's pastime defined by Zora Neale Hurston as "a sort of aimless talking. A man half seriously flirts with a girl, half seriously threatens to fight or brags of his prowess in love, battle, or in financial matters."[2] Lending a spice to the woofing is the female blues banter that (sometimes through a simple change in gender) can provide ammunition for a male put-down:

You can never tell what's on a country man's mind
He'll be huggin' and kissin' you but quittin' you all the time.

Sara Martin: *Mama's Got The Blues*: 1922

---

1 Another old proverb, "Cheer up; there ain't no hell", enlightens Son House on the subject of death: "Oh there ain't no heaven, ain't no burnin' hell; Where I'm goin' when I die, can't nobody tell."
2 Zora Neale Hurston: *Mules and Men*: Harper and Row reprint of the 1935 edition: New York: 1970: p. 305. An arch woofer was Charlie Patton, to judge by Son House's description of him: "He'd take all them old foolish songs and things . . . that's the way he played; he'd just say anything, the first thing he could think of . . ."

You can't never tell what's on a good woman's mind
You might think she's crazy about you, she's leavin' you all the time.

Blind Lemon Jefferson: *Got The Blues:* 1926

As one is now prepared to expect, the line between the eclecticism, self-expression, and whimsicality of country blues couplets concerning women is so fickle that it is the mentality of the artist, not his lovers, that begs scrutiny. Nor would this matter, were it not for the fact that an insight into women's ways is probably the only "folk wisdom" he truly cherishes.

The least ambiguous and most self-revealing blues verses deal with travel, a theme so dominant that blues might have been better named "the jumps". The country blues panorama is basically a railroad depot, though the artist neither sentimentalizes the train nor the traveler in bluegrass or ballad fashion. He simply travels. Some songs are deliberately contrived as the dialogue of a person in transit, as when Barefoot Bill concludes his *Squabblin' Blues* with the remark: ". . . it's train time now, said I reckon I better go", as though what had preceded had been a hobo's anecdote. Here art imitates life; as one musician described the blues life to Gayle Wardlow: "You'd get ready to go in the country at that time . . . you'd come to town. And you play a piece or two; let the people know which-a-way you're goin'. Then you take off."

The popular image of the country bluesman as a nomadic figure is paralleled by now-forgotten racial lore about the Southern black. Before the advent of passenger trains in Mississippi blacks were noted for their fondness for excursion boats, such as occasionally figure in blues couplets. Mark Twain wrote in 1880:

> These poor people could never travel when they were slaves; so they make up for the privation now. They stay on a plantation till the desire to travel seizes them; then they pack up, hail a steamboat, and clear out. Not for any particular place; no, nearly any place will answer; they only want to be moving. The amount of money on hand will answer the rest of the conundrum for them. If it will take them fifty miles, very well; let it be fifty. If not, a shorter flight will do. [1]

A belief in the basic rootlessness of the black was one of the key reasons Mississippi politicians wrote a residency requirement into the voting provision of the 1890 state constitution that ushered in Jim Crow rule. Some of the earliest Jim Crow legislation enforced segregation on railways; a touring Englishman who observed that blacks "love hanging around railway stations" supported this maneuver as a means of protecting the traveler from "a miscellaneous multitude of the Negro race." [2] In general, whites believed that blacks were better left at home, and that traveling on their part was a bit of self-indulgence. As Ray Baker wrote in 1908: "The 'moving about' instinct is strong in all Negroes—sometimes to their destruction." [3]

That this alleged instinct sometimes worked to the destruction of planters with crop liens had much to do with such solicitude; the "instinct" itself probably had equally to do with the sterility of the plantation system and its short-term contractual hold on labor. From his planter's perspective an Alfred Stone could do no more than decry black waywardness, a subject he hammered home before the American Economic Association in a series of turn-of-the-century lectures:

> The desire to move from place to place, the absence of a local attachment, seems to be a governing trait in the Negro character, and a most unfortunate one for the race. It has led to the fixed conviction on the part of many people having constant business relations with him that in this respect the Negro cannot be depended upon at all . . .
>
> To my mind they (blacks) are a restless people. Ever seeking change, they sometimes wander far afield . . . they move but in a narrow cir

1 *Life On The Mississippi*: Lancer Books: 1968: p. 276.
2 William Archer: *Through Anglo-America*: Chapman and Hall, Ltd: London: 1910: p. 69.
3 *Following The Color Line*: Harper and Row edition: New York: 1964: p. 90.

cle, yet always in the same vain, aimless quest . . . Certainly, the plantation Negro changes his residence far too often for his children to form local attachments or to develop anything akin to such a sentiment.

There is no way of computing the amount expended by them in railway travel alone, but it is an enormous sum. This travel is for the most part entirely aimless, and it is a common thing for a Negro to take a trip from a plantation to a town fifteen miles distant, with bare train fare in his pocket, and a crop badly in need of his attention at home.

The country bluesman's insight into what (probably unbeknownst to him) had become a social issue is negligible inasmuch as he enacts the role of traveler. In dramatizing travel it is a blues convention to rationalize this activity as a consequence of a sour love affair or as an effort to shake off the "blues":

I got to keep movin'; I got to keep movin';
blues fallin' down like hail . . .

She walked down the yard, caught the longest train she seen
She said she'd ride till "the blues wear offa me."

Woman takes the blues, she gonna buy her paper and read
Man take the blues he gonna catch a train and leave.

Often departure itself triggers off fits of dejection, not only on the part of the forsaken artist but on the part of his own grass widows as well. It is said by back-slapping blues commentators that the form covers the entire spectrum of human emotion, but it is difficult to recollect a couplet whereby a song character is unmoved by (or actually welcomes) abandonment.

Nor does country blues verse quite capture the violence and insatiability of wanderlust as it presented itself to Booker White, a Mississippi bluesman who recorded his own tribute to freight trains, and remembers: ". . . When a train holler I'd almost jump outta my skin. When you get in love with a freight train, I'm tellin' you the truth—you can be walkin' along the road somewhere, as far as that freight train 'holler'—you gonna tell the peoples excuse you; you gone—you just can't stand it . . .

"I used to be on my way somewhere and then swear Almighty God I wasn't goin' nowhere; be on my way from the church with my girl-friend; we'd be talkin'. And when one of them old freight trains holler there— 'Ooooh-ooooh!'—I said: 'You-all 'scuse me . . .'. I'd go catch that freight train. They wouldn't see me the next two-three years.

"Man, I'd slip *off*, honest to *God* I'd slip off; I'd be *gone*. And the next time I seen 'em, they said: 'You tell me *two years ago*, you told me excuse you, *what happened to you?*'

"I said: 'Well . . . I just caught the train.'

"They said: 'You just nuts!'

"I just couldn't help it. Look like the whistle'll draw me; I don't know. And don't let me get the scent of that smoke! I *had* to leave then. I'm tellin' you the truth. I just had the 'Hobo blues', that's all. I just couldn't stand it, man."

Academic curiosity about country blues could have long ago provided an antidote to the notions that the "folk life" of Southern blacks consisted of a succession of animal fables and gospel trains, and that the inner life of the same group formed a vacuum. A like curiosity about Southern blacks and their cultural background should now give pause to glib critical assertions about country blues. If nothing else, a consideration of the materials they brought to bear in creating blues dispels an archaic perception of the plantation black as "Original in act and thought/Because unlearned and untaught", as Irwin Russell described them in the first successful racial dialect poem, *Christmas Night In The Quarters*. The current tendency to uncritically certify (and glamorize) country blues as existential self-expression or poetry only reflects this view of rural blacks as noble savage-savants working in a cultural void. The intellectual father of the idea that "folk" expression is poetic is Wordsworth, whose idealization of the peasant as a poetic speaker degenerated into a form of salesmanship for the nineteenth century ballad. In America this appreciation of folk music was probably first applied to black spirituals, which a white Southerner commended as early as 1859 for their "simple and poetic images".[1] It neatly complemented the barbaric image of the slave, for poetry had been equated with cultural primivity some three decades earlier by the maxim of Macaulay: "The vocabulary of an enlightened society is philosophical, that of a half-civilized people is poetical."

Of late the word "poetry" has become a sop to confer academic respectability upon non-intellectual verse. We now have the poetry of rock, the poetry of the nursery rhyme, and the poetry of the Old Testament. That we should need to declaim the poetry of country blues in order to esteem it attests to our complete removal from its own sensibility. It is only too clear that neither fine phrases nor fine dissections of country blues can ever bridge the barriers of time, place, class, and race that separate its lyrics from their present audience. But fortunately, country blues also speaks a dialect that may be more compelling and more eloquent than its own verbal statements: the rhythmic body English that derails the senses as the freight train scrambled Booker White's. Over a century ago, Olmsted moved in spite of himself in "instinctive bodily sympathy" to the rhythmic exhortation of a black pastor whose text he could scarcely decode, let alone recall afterwards. Forty years ago the Delta barrelhouse audience of Charlie Patton vibrated in assent to the manner in which his feet and guitar "talked" along with the verses that were difficult for even live listeners to penetrate through his exotic drawl. Today country blues often moves the listener no less, and one could require no more of it.

—Stephen Calt
September, 1972

1 Edward A. Pollard: *Black Diamonds Gathered In The Darkey Homes Of The South*: Pudney and Russell: New York: 1859: p. 35. A somewhat similar appreciation was evinced by Harriet Beecher Stowe: ". . . The Negro mind, impassioned and imaginative, always attaches itself to hymns and expressions of a vivid and pictorial nature . . ."

About Blues Music

This article gives you an understanding of the methods employed in country blues music. I try to make the music as simple as possible. It is important to understand the purpose of the music, which is secondary to the verbal expression of what a blues singer has to say. The blues, in other words, is simply the most natural means of this expression. My approach to the analyzation of the music will be a traditional one. I include a brief note on each of the essential musical elements. Within each, there is mentioned specific characteristics common to all the songs in this book.

Blues is a very natural musical form of expression. A blues chorus is generally twelve measures long, divided into three call and response sections, yielding an overall scheme of A A B. Some blues tunes are contracted to an eight measure form, others are expanded to sixteen or even twenty-four measure forms. These less common forms of eight, sixteen, and twenty-four measures are usually simple variations of the basic twelve measure pattern.

In some early blues tunes, form is unstandardized and approximate. There are examples where a blues will not fall into a conventional twelve measure pattern. The addition of words, either spoken or sung, or the addition of instrumental accompaniment fills, extends the form. This accounts for some of the unusual thirteen or fourteen measure blues melodies. This also works the other way. The twelve bar pattern may also appear shortened to ten or eleven measures through omission of rests. This generally takes place at emotional peaks where a singer is simply in a hurry to get on to the next phrase.

In some cases these irregularities have been omitted in lead sheets. In other cases they have been included. Each situation is dependent on overall form and the strength of a singer's performance.

The singer delivers a statement over the first two or more measures filling the remainder of a phrase with fill-in accompaniment figures; fill-ins act as a set up for the second stanza, which is generally a repetition of the first two measures. Sometimes the second phrase is ornamented with pick-ups such as ". . . and I" or ". . . well it's . . .", or with answers such as "yea" or "baby". The third stanza is a contrasting musical statement which generally resolves or recapitulates the thought in the first and second stanzas.

The following diagram will help you to understand the format of the blues. It shows the structural levels at which one hears the form.

Full Tune											
Each Chorus	(1)						(2)				
Phrases	A		A		B		A		A		B
Motives (Call and Response)	C	R	C	R	C	R	C	R	C	R	C	R
Each Measure	1 2 3 4 5 6 7 8 9 10 11 12						1 2 3 4 5 6 7 8 9 10 11 12				

The rhythmic aspect of country blues music is much like most forms of jazz. There is a certain feeling in which a singer phrases his melodies. This feeling is one of forward propelling motion, and a certain type of accentuation with which notes are played and sung. Syncopation plays an important part in the music, the accentuation of other than natural pulsations (beats 1,2,3, and 4). It is the equilibrium between syncopation and the reinforcement of the basic rhythmic pulsation together with an overall behind the time feeling which characterizes most of the music.

The basic rhythmic feeling is generally represented in the accompaniment. Many times there is a heavy back beat feeling achieved through accentuation of beats two and four. The vocal melody line will vary in its intricacy. In many cases there is much irregularity. At times this is due to the spontaneity of vocal interpretations. Singers would take many liberties with rhythm, especially if they had something to add in the form of words or rhythmic fills.

Most of the songs are written in $\frac{4}{4}$ (𝄴) or cut time (𝄵). In all cases there is a feeling of triple sub-division of each beat. The basic four-four pattern:

does have an underlying feeling of:

Many music theorists have used twelve-eight time ($\frac{12}{8}$) to express this feeling:

is equal to:

This sub-division concept is very important to the understanding of jazz eighth notes. They are not equal as in traditional music. The first eighth note in each group of two is longer than the second.

Traditional interpretation of eighth notes:

All played or sung evenly.

Jazz interpretation of eighth notes:

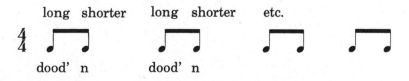

This comes from the underlying triple sub-division:

If written out exactly, the jazz eighth note feeling would be as follows:

In all cases, written eighth notes are to be interpreted as above, except where otherwise noted.

There are certain irregularities in regard to the coordination between rhythmic values and words. Other than the common use of one word to one note, two other possibilities arise:

1. One word equal to more than one note.

I've _____

The dash indicates the continuation of the vocal sound over the written rhythm.

2. One note equal to more than one word.

I've been

Usually the words have been slurred together.

In these cases the second word is not articulated.

The following are examples of some of the commonly used rhythmic articulations found in lead sheets:

long—full value   moderately short

very short   with a heavy accent

The use of the word harmony in my analysis applies primarily to the chord progressions used. There are very few instances of harmonizations of melodies in country blues music. The blues revolves around the use of three primary chords:

   I — Tonic
  IV — Sub-dominant
   V — Dominant

These tonal areas are distributed over the 12 bar blues form. Because of the possibilities for countless variations of the harmonic form, most of the lead sheets include the chords in their simplest variations.

This is the blues harmonic form:

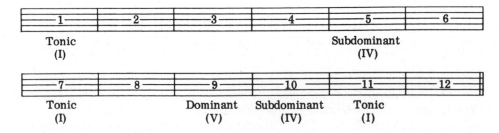

The above is shown using basic triads which in many cases are extended to their 7th.

In order to understand the overall harmonic form it is best to break it down into its 3 sections: A — A — B.

The first "A" section revolves around the tonic chord. Included within this section is the call and response over the first two measures, followed by a lead-in fill over the 3rd and 4th measures.

There are two variations on the basic form. Instead of continuing the basic triad for the full four measure duration, the first expansion would simply add the flatted 7th in the 4th measure. This creates a strong tendency to go onward.

The second variation adds the sub-dominant IV7 in the second measure.

This is particularly effective because the harmonic change occurs on the response to the first call.

The second four measures contains the sub-dominant for two (2) measures, during which time the call and response is repeated. This returns to the tonic in measure seven (7) for two more.

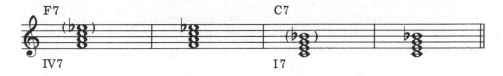

The last "B" section which starts in the 9th measure will be dominant, or sub-dominant, or an interchanging of the two, which returns to the tonic in measure #11. This is the sum-up of the two (2) previous call and response patterns.

Some of the common variations are:

The 12th measure* will remain tonic or change to the dominant or sub-dominant in order to increase the tendency to return to the beginning. There are, of course, countless variations of the basic blues chord changes. Most of country blues music uses the simplest of harmonies. Other forms such as the rag are more harmonically complex, and for this reason are less desirable to the performer. The blues harmonies leave plenty of room for individual expression.

Because of the many possibilities for distribution of the various chord structures, there are many instances where harmonies would vary throughout a tune. This accounts for chord changes which are parenthesized, (F7). Any chord symbol in parenthesis means it is not always present. The performer would stagger its use from chorus to chorus.

Blues melodies are characterized by a distinctly different sound than that of a diatonic major tonality. This is achieved through the superimposition of blues notes on a major scale.

Major scale:

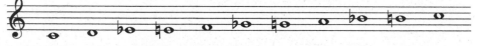

Blues notes are:

In combination:

The distinctive characteristic of European tonal music is the major scale and the presence of two very strong notes, the 4th and the 7th, and the strong resolutional tendencies to 3 and 8 respectively:

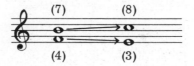

These tonal characteristics are not as important in blues music because of the presence of the ♭3 and ♭7. They are more flexible tones and therefore make for a less restricting tonal sound. The use of the pentatonic scale has come up quite frequently for this reason. The excluded *3 & 7* in pentatonic tonality explains its adaptability to a variety of musical styles, most commonly in folk music. With the addition of the ♭3 and ♭7 (sometimes the ♭5) we also come up with another commonly used scale:

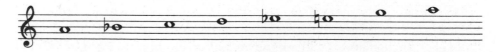

In frequent cases the pitch axis of the pentatonic scale is changed from one to six, thus giving us another familiar sound common to blues tonality.

Blues notes will often times vary in their intonation. Some notes are commonly sung very flat to achieve a "blues sound". There are many instances of slides between notes and the bending of pitches. There are a few basic articulations which have been used to express these techniques.

1. *The bend*—shown as a short curved line prior to the actual note. This means that the note varies in its intonation; most commonly starts flat and gradually raises pitch:

2. *Connecting glissandos and slides*—are either:
       a. articulated—jagged line connecting two notes through the use of approximate scale tones.
       b. unarticulated—straight line connecting two notes but no individual pitches are heard.

Examples:

Blues singers employ two melodic techniques over the first two "A" phrases:

    1. Transposition: repeating a melodic phrase at another pitch level (usually from tonic to sub-dominant):

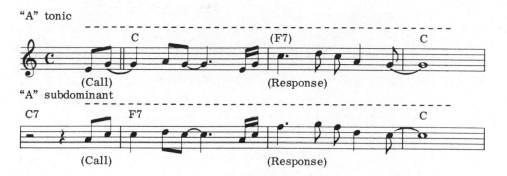

    2. Superimposition: use of same set of pitches on a different chord (again usually from tonic to sub-dominant):

These are the primary characteristics of the "A" phrases. The final "B" phrase is usually different in character. It's usually a concluding statement and often times less "bluesy" sounding because it must resolve the previous phrases.

Country blues' style most commonly appears in the form of a man singing his story while accompanying himself on his unamplified guitar. Many times there are spoken segments, usually during introductions and endings. In addition to his vocalizations the country blues singer would occasionally express his instrumental capacities in the form of single string guitar solos and fills. Sometimes other instruments might appear functioning in an accompanying capacity. Commonly used additional instruments include: harmonica, jug, kazoo, washboards, fiddle, bass, and sometimes even piano.

This article is by no means a complete analysis of country blues music. It should, however, acquaint you with the basic ingredients contained within the realm of blues music, and in doing so, further your overall understanding of this musical art form.

—Hal Grossman

Fallin' Down Blues

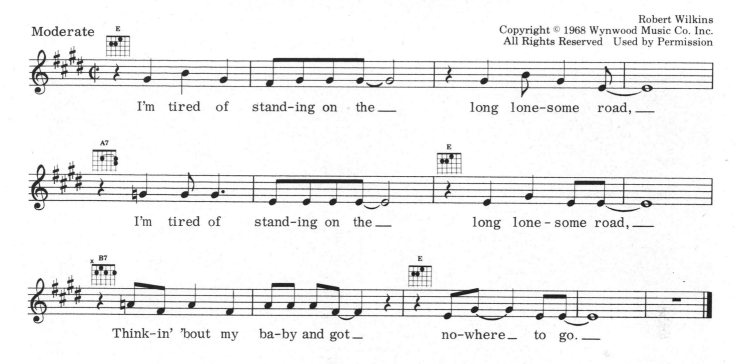

I'm tired of standin' on the long lonesome road, (twice)
Thinkin' 'bout my baby and got nowhere to go.

It's as far down the road, friend, as I can see,
It's as far down the road, friend, as I can see,
See the woman I love standin' wavin' after me.

I run to her, friend, fell down at her knee, (twice)
Cryin', "Take me back, baby, God knows, if you please."

If you don't believe, girl, I'll treat you right, (twice)
Come and walk with me down to my lovin' shack tonight.

I'll certainly treat you just like you was white,* (twice)
That don't satisfy you, girl, I'll take your life.

I love you, girl, I will tell the world I do, (twice)
And that's the reason you treat me like you do.†

But go ahead, girl, that will be all right for you, (twice)
I will meet you someday when you're down in hard luck, too.

*I.e., deferentially
†This remarks on the imagined perversity of women, a favorite
 subject of bluesmen. According to the conventional blues wisdom,
 a woman is apt to repay kindness with abuse and abuse with
 gratitude.

Drunken Spree

Skip James
Copyright © 1965 Wynwood Music Co. Inc.
All Rights Reserved   Used by Permission

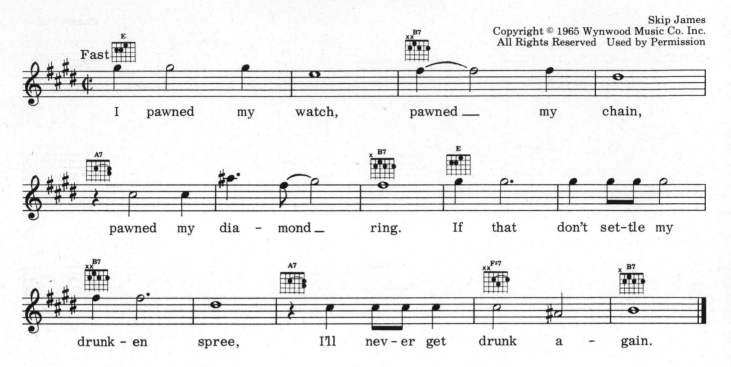

I pawned my watch, pawned ___ my chain, pawned my dia - mond ___ ring. If that don't set-tle my drunk - en spree, I'll nev - er get drunk a - gain.

I pawned my watch, pawned my chain,
Pawned my diamond ring.
If that don't settle my drunken spree,
I'll never get drunk again.

It was late last night when Miss Willie
    come home,
She'd made one rap on my door.
I said, "Is that you, Miss Willie? I'd like
    to know.
Don't you rap no more."

I love Miss Willie, yes I do,
I love her till the sea go dry.
And if I thought she didn't love me,
I'd take morphine and die.

She's up in her little stockin' feet, tippin'
    'cross the floor,
Just like she had done before.
Yes, and I pawned my clothes, pawned my shoe,
I'll never get drunk no more. . . .

I begged Miss Willie, down on my knee,
To forgive me, if she please.
"Well, you done caused me to weep and you
    caused me to moan,
Done caused me to lose my happy home."

I hollered, "Oh me, oh my,
I'll never let another drink go by."
If I thought she didn't love me,
I'd take morphine and die.

I pawned my watch, pawned my chain,
Pawned my diamond ring.
And if that don't settle all my drunken spree,
Lord, I'll never get drunk again.

44

Down The Dirt Road

Charlie Patton

I'm goin' a - way to a world — un - known. _____

I'm goin' a - way_____ to a world un - known. _____

I'm wor-ried now, ____ but I ____ won't be wor-ried long. ____

I'm goin' away to a world unknown,
I'm goin' away to a world unknown,
I'm worried now, but I won't be worried long.

My rider got somethin', she's tryin'a keep it hid,
My rider got somethin', she's tryin'a keep it hid,
Lord, I got somethin' to find that somethin' with.

I feel like choppin', chips flyin' everywhere,
I feel like choppin', chips flyin' everywhere,
I been to the Nation,* oh Lord, but I couldn't stay there.

Some people tell me them oversea blues ain't bad,
(*Spoken:* Why, of course they are)
Some people say them oversea blues ain't bad,
(*Spoken:* What was a-matter with 'em?!)
It must not a-been them oversea blues I had.

Every day seem like murder here,
(*Spoken:* My God, I'm no sheriff)
Every day seem like murder here,
I'm gonna leave tomorrow, I know you don't bid my care.

Can't go down any dirt road by myself,
Can't go down any dirt road by myself,
(*Spoken:* My Lord, who you gonna carry?)
I don't carry my (rider?), gonna carry me someone else.

Nation: The "Indian Nation" now Oklahoma; a nineteenth-
century term.

Bud Russell Blues*

Sam Hopkins
Copyright © 1971 Tradition Music Co.
All Rights Reserved   Used by Permission

Spoken Introduction:

Sho' is hot out here. Bud Russell don't care. He said he didn't send for me and he didn't ask me to come down here, for this is *Penitentiara*.

Lord, you oughta been on Big Brazos, oh man, nineteen hundred and ten,
Yeah, you oughta been on Big Brazos (*spoken:* Lord have mercy), young man,
    nineteen hundred and ten,
You know, Bud Russell drove pretty womens, just like he did them ugly mens.

*In this song, the dramatic reminiscence of an old convict, Bud Russell is an overseer or a
  section boss.

Yeah, you know, my mama called me one mornin', I answered, "Ma'am?"
"Son, are you tired o' workin'?" I told her, "Mama, yes I am."
Then my papa called me, I answered, "Sir?"
"Son, if you tired o' workin', what in the hell you gonna stay down here for?"†
Man, that was in nineteen hundred and ten,
You know, Bud Russell drove them pretty womens, just like he did them ugly mens.
(*Spoken:* An' I was one of 'em.)

Spoken prelude to third vocal verse:
I had to ask the question and I wanted to have it like I wanted.

Please take care of my wife and child, I mean I'll 'turn back to my home life,
Please take care of my wife and child, I mean I'll 'turn back to my home life.
You know, the next time the bossman hit me I'm, I'm gonna give him a big surprise.
(*Spoken:* I ain't jokin', neither.)

Spoken Conclusion:
I'm goin' home one of these old rainy days.

†In this dialogue between the narrator and his parents, "working" refers to prison labor.

From Four Until Late

Robert Johnson

From four____ un-til late____ I was wring-in' my hands an' cry - in'.

From four____ un-til late____ I was wring-in' my hands____ an' cry - in'.

I be - lieve to my soul that your dad - dy's Gulf____ port bound.____

From four until late I was wringin' my hands an' cryin',
From four until late I was wringin' my hands an' cryin'.
I believe to my soul that your daddy's Gulfport bound.

From Memphis to Norfolk is a thirty-six hours' drive,
From Memphis to Norfolk is a thirty-six hours' ride.
A man is like a prisoner, and he's never satisfied.

A woman is like a dresser, some man always ramblin' through its drawer,
A woman is like a dresser, some man's always ramblin' through its drawer.
It caused so many men wearin' apron overalls.*

From four until late, she give us a no-good bartend' clown,
From four until late, she give us a no-good bartend' clown.
Now, and she won't do nothin' but tear a good man's reputation down.

When I leave this town, I'm gonna bid you fare-farewell,
And when I leave this town, I'm gonna bid you fare-farewell.
An' when I return again, you'll have a great long story to tell.

*With this verse Johnson seems to suggest that men are forced to support
 women in order to gratify their own sexual urges.

Knockin' Down Windows

Mance Lipscomb
Copyright © 1970 Tradition Music Co.
All Rights Reserved   Used by Permission

Goin' up-town, _ what do you want me to bring you back? _

Yes, I'm goin' up-town, _ what do you want me to bring you back? _

— I was knock-in' down win-dows, tear-

in' down doors, _ Tryin' to get e-ven with the girl I love...

Guitar:

Goin' uptown, what do you want me to bring you back?
Yes, I'm goin' uptown, what do you want me to bring you back?
I was knockin' down windows, tearin' down doors,
Tryin' to get even with a girl I love. . . .

A brownskin woman make a preacher lay his Bible down,
Tell me, a brownskin woman'll make a preacher lay his Bible down.
I'm both knockin' down windows, was tearin' around doors,
Tryin' to get even with a girl I love.
Brownskin woman'll make a preacher lay his Bible down.

An' a jet-black woman'll make a rabbit hug a hound,
An' a jet-black woman'll make a rabbit hug a hound.
Knockin' down windows, was tearin' around doors,
Was tryin' to get even with a girl I love.
. . . Make a rabbit hug a hound.

Oh, that's my girl, 'cause she got good curly hair,
Oh, she's my girl and she got good curly hair.
I been knockin' down windows and tearin' down doors,
Just tryin' to get even with a girl I love. . . .

Well, a brownskin woman'll get anything I got,
Well, a brownskin woman, she can get anything I got.
And a jet-black girl can't go in my house lot.

You can knock me down, I'm a-slow drag* up again,
You can knock me down, I'm a-slow drag up again.
Oh, I was knockin' down windows and tearin' around doors,
Was tryin' to get even with a girl I love. . . .

*The comparison is to a blues dance called the slow drag.

Risin' River Blues

George Carter

Risin' river blues runnin' by my door, (twice)
They're runnin', sweet mama, like they haven't done before.

I got to move in the alley, I ain't allowed on the street, (twice)
These risin' river blues sure have got me beat.

Third verse hummed.

Come here, sweet mama, let me speak my mind, (twice)
To cure these blues, gonna take a long, long time.

Devil Got My Woman

. . . The devil was stronger than I was, an' he did have, and is got now, a certain amount of power . . . And he lives in Hell, and that's where he haves his part. And God give him a certain amount of time to be on the earth, in the bowels, persuadin' people . . . He still have agencies out. Everywhere you've been. And then he's a man don't never sleep. He never get offa his job or duty. That is, you can lay down happy at night, you and your companion . . . and in harmony. Everything goin' well. Satan'll creep in the house overnight . . . next mornin' you cannot get a good word out of her. Why? Because Satan has got the bill of sale over her. He done crept in overnight . . .

——Skip James

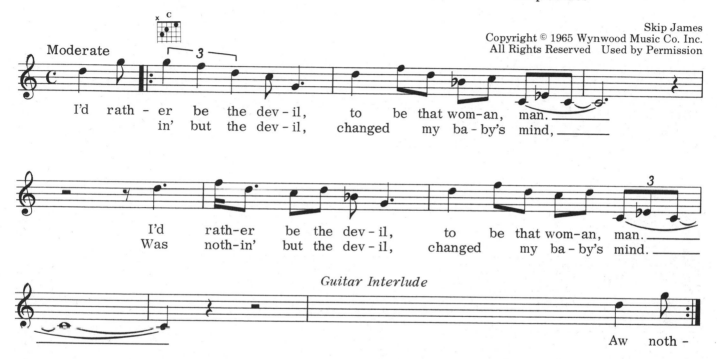

I'd rather be the devil, to be that woman man,*
I'd rather be the devil, to be that woman man.
Aw, nothin' but the devil changed my baby's mind,
Was nothin' but the devil changed my baby's mind.

I laid down last night, laid down last night,
I laid down last night, tried to take my rest.
My mind got to ramblin', like a wild geese
From the west, from the west.

The woman I loved, woman that I loved,
Woman I loved, took her from my best friend,
But he got lucky, stoled her back again,
And he got lucky, stoled her back again.

*James usually completed this line with "woman's man."

I Ain't Goin' Cry No More

Son House
Copyright © 1942 by Sondick Music Company
All Rights Reserved   Used by Permission

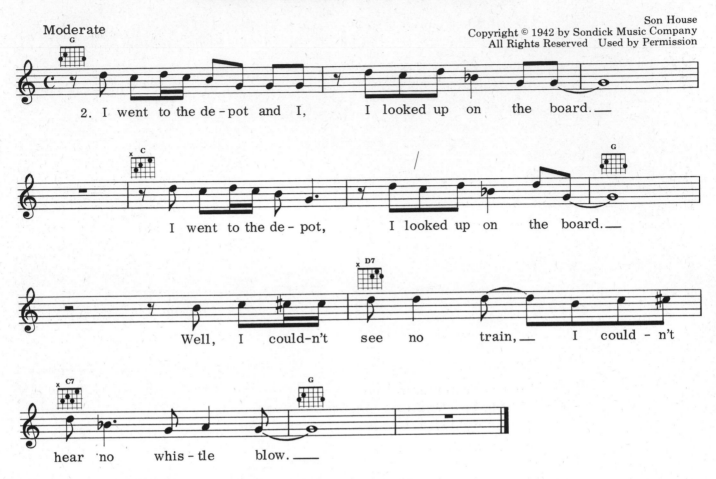

First line hummed
Well, lookey here, honey, I ain't gonna cry no more.

I went to the depot and I, I looked up on the board,
I went to the depot, I looked up on the board.
Well, I couldn't see no train, I couldn't hear no whistle blow.

Engineer blowed the whistle and the fireman, he rung the bell,
Oh, oh, the fireman, he rung the bell.
You know, my woman was on board, she was wavin' back, "Fare you well."

If I had any strength, I would set this train off the track,
. . . I would set this train off the track.
Else you make me a promise, you gonna bring my baby back.*

. . . you ain't comin' back no more,
I don't believe you ever comin' back no more.
You leavin' now, baby, bet you hangin' creper† on my door.

I'm gonna miss you from rollin' in my arms,
I'm gonna miss you from rollin' in my arms.
If I can't get no stamps and paper, I'm gonna sit down and telephone.

*Rhetorically, this line is addressed to the train and its crew.
†*creper:* crepe, a hackneyed symbol of mourning. The woman in question would post it, in House's imagination, to declare the death of her feelings for him.

Cypress Grove Blues

Skip James
Copyright © 1965 Wynwood Music Co. Inc.
All Rights Reserved   Used by Permission

I would rath-er be bur - ied   in some cy - press grove,

I would rath-er be bur - ied   in some cy - press grove;

to have some wom-an, —   Lord, that I can con - trol. —

I would rather be buried in some cypress grove,
I would rather be buried in some cypress grove,
To have some woman, Lord, that I can't control.

And I'm goin' away now, I'm goin' away to stay,
And I'm goin' away now, I'm goin' away to stay,
That'll be all right, pretty mama, you gonna need my help someday.

And the sun goin' down, and you know what your promise means,
And the sun goin' down, you know what your promise means,
And what's the matter, baby, I can't see.

I would rather be dead and six feet in my grave,
I would rather be dead and six feet in my grave,
Than to be way up here, honey, treated this a-way.

And the old people told me, baby, but I never did know,
The old people told me, baby woman, but I never did know,
"The Good Book declare you got to reap just what you sow."

When your knee bone's achin' and your body cold,
When your knee bone's achin' and your body cold,
Means you just gettin' ready, honey, for the cypress grove.

Shake It And Break It

Charlie Patton

You can shake it you can break it you can hang it on the wall,

Throw it out the win-dow, — catch it 'fore it roll. You can

shake it you can break it you can hang it on the wall,

It out the win-dow, catch it 'fore it falls. My

jel-ly, my roll; sweet ma-ma don't let it fall.

Chorus:

Ev-'ry-bod-y have a jel-ly roll like mine; I lives in town.

I ain't got no brown, I; an' I want it now. My

jel-ly, my roll; sweet ma-ma don't let it fall.

You can shake it, you can break it, you can hang it on the wall,
Throw it out the window, catch it 'fore it roll.
You can shake it, you can break it, you can hang it on the wall,
. . . it out the window, catch it 'fore it falls.
My jelly, my roll, sweet mama, don't let it fall.

Chorus:
Everybody have a jelly roll like mine, I lives in town,
I—ain't got no brown, I—an' I want it now.
My jelly, my roll, sweet mama, don't let it fall.

You can snatch it, you can grab it, you can break it, you can twist it,
Any way that I love to get it.
I—had my right mind since I—I blowed this town,
My jelly, my roll, sweet mama, don't let it fall.

Jus' shake it, you can break it, you can hang it on the wall,
. . . it out the window, catch it 'fore it falls.
You can break it, you can hang it on the wall,
. . . it out the window, catch it 'fore it . . .
My jelly, my roll, sweet mama, don't let it fall.

Chorus:
I ain't got nobody here but me and myself,
I—stay blue all the time, aw, when the sun goes down.
My jelly, my roll, sweet mama, don't let it fall.

You can shake it, you can break it, you can hang it on the wall,
. . . it out the window, catch it 'fore it fall.
You can break it, you can hang it on the wall,
. . . it out the window, catch . . .
My jelly, my roll, sweet mama, don't let it fall.

You can snatch it, you can grab it, you can break it, you can twist it,
Any way that I love to get it.
I—had my right mind, I—be worried sometime,
'Bout a jelly, my roll, sweet mama, don't let it fall.

Just shake it, you can break it, you can hang it on the wall,
. . . it out the window, catch it 'fore it falls.
You can break it, you can hang it on the wall,
. . . it out the window, catch it 'fore it falls.
My jelly, my roll, sweet mama, don't let it fall.

Chorus:
I know I been to town, I—I walked around.
I—start leavin' town, I—I fool around.
My jelly, my roll, sweet mama, don't let it fall.

Just shake it, you can break it, you can hang it on the wall,
. . . it out the window, catch it 'fore it falls.
You can break it, you can hang it on the wall,
. . . it out the window, catch it 'fore it . . .
My jelly, my roll, sweet mama, don't let it fall.

Chorus:
Jus' shake it, you can break it, you can hang it on the wall,
. . . it out the window, catch it 'fore it . . .
My jelly, my roll, sweet mama, don't let it . . .

Devil In The Lion's Den

Sam Collins

My ma-ma's dead and __ my pa-pa can't __ be found. __

My ma - ma's dead __ and my pa-pa __ can't be found.

I ain't got me no - bod-y, throw my arms a - round. __

My mama's dead and my papa can't be found,
My mama's dead and my papa can't be found,
I ain't got me nobody throw my arms around.

Yon come the devil, gonna set this town on fire,
Yon come the devil, gonna set this town on fire,
'Low me a chance, come darkness, to bid this town good-bye.

I got ways like a devil, sleep in the lion's den,
I got ways like a devil, sleep in a lion den,
If I can find me a good gal I'm gonna take her hand.

Let me tell you, mama, what you said last night,
Let me tell you, mama, what you said last night,
Lay down on my bedside, tried to treat me right.

Lord, I'm goin' up the country, your cryin' won't make me stay,
I'm goin' up the country, cryin' won't make me stay,
The more you cry, the further I'll ride away.

Crossroad Blues

Robert Johnson

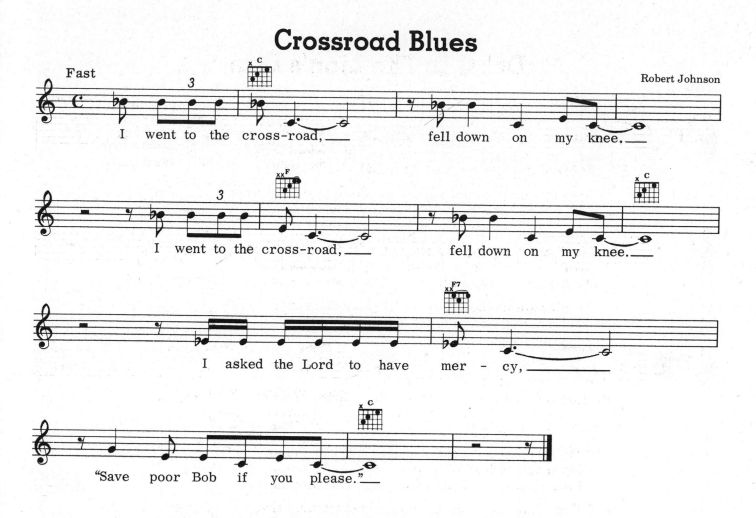

I went to the crossroad, fell down on my knee,
I went to the crossroad, fell down on my knee,
I asked the Lord to have mercy, "Save poor Bob, if you please."

Standin' at the crossroad, I tried to flag a ride,
Standin' at the crossroad, I tried to flag a ride,
Didn't nobody seem to know me, everybody passed me by.

And the sun's goin' down, boy, dark gonna catch me here,
. . . boys, dark gonna catch me here,
I haven't got no lovin' sweet woman left, (to) love an' feel my care.

You can run, you can run, tell my friend-boy Willie Brown,*
You can run, tell my friend-boy Willie Brown,
Lord, that I'm standin' at the crossroad, baby, I believe I'm sinkin' down.

*Willie Brown (q.v.) was Johnson's neighbor and musical associate in Robin-
sonville, Mississippi, during the latter's formative years in the early thirties.

Coffee Blues

Mississippi John Hurt
Copyright © 1963 Wynwood Music Co. Inc.
All Rights Reserved   Used by Permission

Medium fast

I've got to go to Mem-phis, bring her back to Le-land.

I want to see my ba-by ____ 'bout a lov-in' spoon-ful,__

My__ lov-in' spoon-ful,

Well, I'm just got to have ____ my lov-in'... (Spoken words)

Spoken:
This is the "Coffee Blues," I likes a certain brand—Maxwell's House—it's good till the last drop, just like it says on the can. I used to have a girl cookin' a good Maxwell House. She moved away. Some said to Memphis and some said to Leland,* but I found her. I wanted her to cook me some good Maxwell's House. You understand, if I can get me just a spoonful† of Maxwell's House, do me much good as two or three cups this other coffee.

I've got to go to Memphis, bring her back
  to Leland,
I wanna see my baby 'bout a lovin' spoonful,
My lovin' spoonful.
Well, I'm just got to have my lovin' ...

Spoken:
I found her.

"Good mornin', baby, how you do this mornin'?
Well, please, ma'am, just a lovin' spoon ...
Just a lovin' spoonful.
I declare, I got to have my lovin' spoonful."

My baby packed her suitcase and she went away,
I couldn't let her stay for my lovin' ...
My lovin' spoonful,
Well, I'm just got to have my lovin' ...

"Good mornin', baby, how you do this mornin'?
Well, please, ma'am, just a lovin' spoon ...
Just a lovin' spoonful,
Well, I'm just got to have my lovin' ..."

Well, the preacher in the pulpit, jumpin'
  up and down,
He laid his Bible down for his lovin' ...
(*Spoken:* Ain't Maxwell House all right?)
Well, I'm just got to have my lovin' ...

Leland: a town in the Mississippi Delta.
†"Spoonful" served as a vague blues euphemism for sex in the traditional "spoonful" song, long before Hurt sprung the "coffee" gag on his audiences. *Cf.* Charlie Patton's "Spoonful Blues."

You can bring me whiskey, you can bring
    me tea,
Nothin' satisfies me, man, but
    my lovin' spoonful,
My lovin' . . .
Well, I'm just got to have my lovin' . . .

"Good mornin' baby, how you do this mornin'?
Well, please, ma'am, just a lovin' . . .
Just a lovin' spoonful."
Makes things all right, with a lovin' . . .

When your baby gets mad and she won't
    do right,
Go to bed at night, get a lovin' . . .
Well, a lovin' spoonful.
Well, I'm just got to have my lovin' . . .

"Good mornin', baby, how you do this mornin'?
Well, please, ma'am, just a lovin' . . ."

Oh, the womens in Greenwood,‡ they raisin' sand,**
It's all about that lovin' . . .
That lovin' spoonful.
I declare, it's all right, that lovin' . . .

‡*Greenwood*: a Mississippi Delta town.
**raisin' sand*: a Southern euphemism for raising hell.

When Your Way Gets Dark

Charlie Patton

Moderate

When your way gets dark ba - by, turn your lights up high.

(Spoken aside:) "What's the matter with 'em?" Where I can see my man, Lord,

if he come eas - in' by.

When your way gets dark, baby, turn your
    lights up high,
(*Spoken:* What's the matter with 'em?)
Where I can see my man, Lord, if he come
    easin' by.

I take my daily,
(*Spoken:* Daily 'fore day prayer!)
I take my daily . . .

Trouble at home, baby,
(*Spoken:* Tryin' to blow me down!)
It wouldn't hurt so bad but the news
    all over this . . .

I love my baby an' I
(*Spoken:* Tell the world I do)
What made me love her, you will come an'
    love her, too.

Hey, someday, baby,
(*Spoken:* You know, an' it won't be long)
You'll call at me, baby, an'—an' I'll be gone.

I'm goin' away, baby,
(*Spoken:* Don't you wanna go?)
I'm goin' away, baby, don't you wanna go?

County Farm Blues

Lyrics by Son House
Music by Blind Lemon Jefferson
(melody from the tune "Two White Horses")
© Copyright 1930 by Olwen Music
All Rights Reserved   Used by Permission

Down South, when you do anything
  that's wrong, (three times)
They'll sure put you down on the county farm.

Put you down under a man they call
  "Captain Jack,"*
Put you under a man called "Captain Jack,"
Put you under a man they call "Captain Jack,"
He'll sure write his name up and down
  your back.

Put you down in a ditch with a
  great long spade, (three times)
Wish to God that you hadn't never been made.

On a Sunday the boys be lookin' sad,
On a Sunday the boys'll be lookin' sad,
On a Sunday the boys be lookin' sad,
Just wonderin' about how much time they had.†

*"Captain" was once one of the forms of address the Southern
  white man demanded from black employees.
†I.e., time left to serve in prison.

Cherry Ball Blues*

Skip James
Copyright © 1965 Wynwood Music Co. Inc.
All Rights Reserved   Used by Permission

I love my cher-ry ball __ bet-ter than I love __ my - self. __

I love my cher-ry ball __ bet-ter than I do __ my - self. __

She get so she don't love me; she won't love no-bod - y else. __

I love my cherry ball better than I love myself,
I loves cherry ball better than I love myself,
She get so she don't love me, she won't love nobody else.

Cherry ball quit me, she quit me in a calm, good way,
Cherry ball quit me, she quit me in a calm, good way,
But what to take to get her, I carries it every day.†

I love my cherry, oh, better than I love myself,
My cherry ball, better than I love myself,
She get so she don't love me, love nobody else.

Sure as that spider hangin' on the wall,
Sure as that spider hangin' on the wall,
I advised that old cherry ball, "Keep fallin' on call."‡

I'll catch the Southern if you take the Santa Fe,
I'll take the Southern and you'll take the Santa Fe,
I'm gonna ride and ramble, tell cherry to come back to me.

*"Cherry ball" is probably blues slang, fostered by the 1930 Memphis
Minnie composition, "Cherry Ball Blues," which begins, "I ain't
gonna give you none o' my cherry ball." James uses it to personify
sex or (according to one's point of view) "dehumanize" women.
†Carrying his boast a step further, James once qualified this couplet
with the remark, "*If* I wanted her, you understand."
‡The advice is to submit sexually on cue.

Sic 'Em Dogs On

. . . A girl made me drunk on that corn whiskey an' she was so nice . . . just made me so welcome, just like my own sister. She said: "Don't you get out in the street, drunk, staggerin'; gonna get arrested . . . You just go right ahead, lay down 'cross that bed. When you wake up, whatever's in your pockets, it'll still be there." And I thanked her . . .

An' when I woke up I didn't have a quarter in my pocket. So I asked her, I said: "Mary, where's my money?"

She said: "How much did you have?"

I said: "I had fifty dollars in my pocket."

She said: "Well, I don't know; ain't nobody been here."

I said: "I *know* ain't nobody been here. *You* the one that got it." And so I called the police.

She had two lil' dogs, one named Butch and one named Fido. An' when I called up the police and I come back, she said: "If you don't leave here I'm gonna sic my dog on ya!" She said: "Sic 'im! Sic 'im! Sic 'im, Butch—Fido won't bite."

. . . Ol' Butch he was a large dog; Fido he was a lil' tyke. An' they jus' ran up on me and growled, you know; they wouldn't try to bite me none.

. . . And so the police tol' her if she didn't give me my money they gonna put her in jail. And when he got over to her to put the handcuffs on her she pulled off her shoe an' give me my fifty dollars . . . An' when she did that, the police said: "Now everything all right? Booker, whatcha do: you go on along home."

I said: "Okay . . ."

Sometimes you can say a thing whatcha wanna do, an' you do the same thing again . . . I was back over there the next week-end.

But I was slick, though: I didn't have but a dollar seventy-five cents in my pocket . . .

An' so we got to drinkin' whiskey (she was sellin' corn whiskey), an' I got high again an' went to lay across the bed an' when I woke up the dollar seventy-five was gone. I didn't say nothin'.

So she fixed dinner for me . . . She had a big ham, an' she had turkey, and she had chicken . . . I know that ham cost more than that other stuff, so I eat about half the ham. An' so I figured that way I got my dollar seventy-five cents back.

I eat so much she told me: "Don't come back no more." She give me the stay-away from her house. She said: "I'm gwine sic the dog on ya. I'm gwine tell you myself: if you ever come back again I'm gwine to put the police on you."

I said: "Don't worry. I got my dollar seventy-five cents, an' I'm goin'."

I never did go back there no more.

—Booker White

Sic 'Em Dogs On

Booker White
Copyright © 1964 Wynwood Music Co. Inc.
All Rights Reserved   Used by Permission

3. You done got my mon-ey now you tried to sic your dog on me. ___

That's all right lit-tle girl how you do me; you go try it a-gain. ___

Says, I'm going downtown and tell the chief police you siccin' your dog on me.

She went runnin', runnin' and cryin',
She said, "Listen, daddy, I ain't gonna do it no more, I ain't gonna do it no more."

You done got my money, now you tried to sic your dog on me.
That's all right, little girl, how you do me, you go try it again.

I'm gonna tell the chief you've got your dog on me, you told me you didn't want me around.
"Oh listen, chief, she's done got all my money, now siccin' her dog on me.

"Chief, when you're runnin' and you cryin' . . ." Don't sic no more an' you call Fido, he won't bite.
If you take me back, I won't do it no more, baby, don't sic your dog on me.

She said, "Listen, daddy, don't you dog me, don't you dog me around."

Crow Jane

... That was deferrin' to some girl what you might call some 'riso-cratic, onery girl friend that you has, and she just figured that she can do you most any kind of way and get by; she got to live forever and never die ... She just want to intrude on you and not be intruded on her personal self ... She's overlookin' you, an' want to use you in a way ... use you as convenience, and every other thing. And she could just live on and live above you and hold her head up above you and ignore you to some extent. And then you give her to know that "some day, *you* got to die."

—Skip James

Crow janie, crow janie, crow jane, don't you
    hold your head high,
Someday, baby, you know you got to die,
You got to lay down and . . .
You got to die, you got to . . .

And I wanna buy me a pistol, wants me
    forty rounds of ball,
Shoot crow jane, just to see her fall,
She got to fall, she got to . . .
She got to fall, she got to . . .

That's the reason I begged crow jane not to
    hold her head so high,
Someday, baby, you know you got to die,
You got to lay down and . . .

And I dug her grave with a silver spade,
Ain't nobody gonna take my crow jane place,
You can't take her place no, you can't
    take her . . .

That's the reason I begged crow jane not to
    hold her head too high,
Someday, baby, you know you got to die,
You got to lay down and . . .

You know, I let her down with a golden chain,
And every link I would call my crow jane name,
Crow jane, crow . . . crow jane, crow . . .

You know, I never missed my water till
    my well went dry,
Didn't miss crow jane until the day she died,
Till the day she . . .

That's the reason I begged crow jane not to
    hold her head too high,
Someday, baby, you know you got to die,
You got to lay down and . . . you got to die,
    you got to . . .

You know, I dug her grave eight feet in
the ground,
I didn't feel sorry until they let her down,
They had to let her down, let her . . . they had
to let her down . . .

That's the reason I begged crow jane not to
hold her head too high,
Someday, baby, you know you got to die,
You got to lay down and . . .

Sugar Babe It's All Over Now

Mance Lipscomb
Copyright © 1968 Tradition Music Co.
All Rights Reserved   Used by Permission

Medium fast

Sug - ar babe, I'm tired of you, — Ain't your hon - ey but the way you do. — Sug-ar babe, — it's all o - ver now. —

Spoken:
It was the first'un I learnt.

Sugar babe, I'm tired of you,
Ain't your honey but the way you do.
Sugar babe, it's all over now.

All I want my babe to do,
Make five dollars and give me two.
Sugar babe, it's all over now.

Went downtown and bought me a rope,
Whupped my baby till she Buzzard Lope.*
Sugar babe, it's all over now.

Sugar babe, what's the matter with you?
You don't treat me like you used to do.
Sugar babe, it's all over now.

Went to town and bought me a line,
Whupped my baby till she changed her mind.
Sugar babe, sugar babe, it's all over now.

Sugar babe, I'm tired of you,
Ain't your honey but the way you do.
Sugar babe, it's all over now.

Buzzard Lope: a solo dance brought to the attention of folklorist
Lydia Parrish as early as 1915, when there was a national vogue
for "animal steps" (the Fox Trot, Camel Walk, Grizzly Bear, etc.).

Cocaine Done Killed My Baby

Mance Lipscomb

Cocaine done killed my baby, cocaine try to run me crazy.
Cocaine gonna kill you after awhile.

I'm goin' away to leave you, I know it's goin' to grieve you.
Cocaine gonna kill you after awhile.

Don't say that I didn't love you, I don't think myself above you.
Cocaine gonna kill you after awhile.

Cocaine done run me crazy, and I tried to kill my baby.
Cocaine kill you after awhile.

Cocaine done run me crazy, I believe gonna kill my baby.
Cocaine gonna kill you after awhile.

I'm goin' away to leave you, it's goin' to grieve you.
Cocaine gonna kill you after awhile.

Don't say that I didn't love you, I don't think myself above you.
Cocaine gonna kill you after awhile.

Catfish

Skip James
Copyright © 1965 Wynwood Music Co. Inc.
All Rights Reserved   Used by Permission

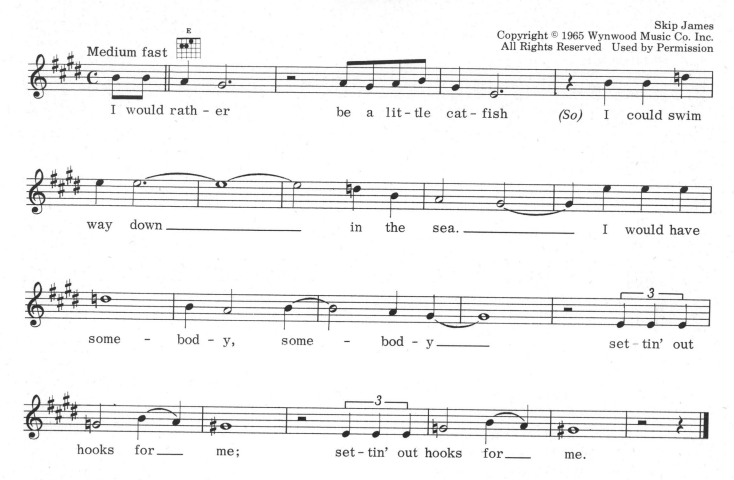

I would rath - er be a lit-tle cat-fish (So) I could swim way down _____ in the sea. _____ I would have some - bod - y, some - bod - y _____ set - tin' out hooks for _____ me; set - tin' out hooks for _____ me.

I would rather be a little catfish
(So) I could swim way down in the sea.
I would have somebody, somebody
Settin' out hooks for me,
Settin' out hooks for me.

You know, I went to my baby's house,
She told me to sit down on the step.
"Son, you can come right on in because my
Husband just now left,
Just now left, just now left."

And I asked my baby to
Let me sit down 'side her bed.
"Turn on your heater
Till they turn cherry red,*
Cherry red, cherry red."

That's the reason I'd ruther be a little catfish,
So I could swim way down in the sea.
I would have many-some of these women
Settin' out a line for me,
Settin' out a line for me, a line for me.

You know, I went to the church house
And they called on me to pray.
I got down on my knees but I didn't
Have no word to say,
Not a word to say, word to say.

That's the reason I'd ruther be a little catfish,
So I could swim way down in the sea.
I would have somebody, somebody
Settin' out a line for me,
Settin' out a line for me, line for me.

I don't wanna be no tadpole,
And I don't wanna be no bullfrog.
And if I can't be a catfish,
I won't swim at all,
I won't swim at all, swim at all.

That's the reason I want to be a little catfish,
So I could swim way down in the sea.
I would have these good-lookin' women
Settin' out a hook for me,
Settin' out a hook for me, hook for me.

*Here the artist bowdlerizes his original phrase, "till your nipples
 turn cherry red."

Sick Bed Blues*

Skip James
Copyright © 1965 Wynwood Music Co. Inc.
All Rights Reserved   Used by Permission

Slow to Moderate

Lay - in' sick, hon - ey, on my bed.___ I'm
lay - in' sick, hon - ey, and on my bed. I'm
lay - in' sick, hon - ey, and on my bed. I used
to have some friends but they wish that I were dead.

Layin' sick, honey, on my bed,
I'm layin' sick, honey, and on my bed, (twice)
I used to have some friends but they wish
    that I were dead.

In awful pain and deep in misery,
Awful pain and deep in misery, (twice)
I ain't got nobody to come and see about me.

And every dog, baby, got a day, (twice)
Every dog, baby, got a day,
But I said, "Please, don't you treat me
    this a-way."

The doctor came, lookin' very sad, (three times)
He diagnosed my case and said it was
    awful bad.
He walked away, mumblin' very low, (three times)
He said, "He may get better but he'll never
    get well no more."

I hollered, "Lord, oh Lord, Lord, Lordie, Lord,
Oh Lordie, Lord, Lord, Lord,
I been so badly misused and treated just
    like a dog."

I've got a long trip and I'm just too weak
    to ride, (twice)
I got a long trip and I'm just too weak to ride,
Now it's a thousand people standin' at
    my bedside.

You take a stone, you can bruise my bone,
You take stone and you can bruise my bone,
You take a stone and you can bruise my bone,
But you sure gonna miss me when I'm
    dead and gone.

I been on the ocean, I been across the sea,
Been on the ocean, I been across the sea, (twice)
I ain't found nobody would feel my sympathy.

*The occasion of this song was James's hospitalization in Tunica, Mississippi, for an apparently undetected cancer, shortly before his "rediscovery" in 1964. Some of the spleen apparent in the verses probably is a result of James's interpretation of his symptoms as the work of a sorceress. Once on the concert circuit, he discarded the piece, because of (so he explained) an aversion to hospitals.

Jinx Blues

Son House
© Copyright 1941 by Sondick Music Company
All Rights Reserved   Used by Permission

First verse hummed.

Well, I got up this mornin', jinx all around, jinx all around, 'round my bed.
And I say I got up this mornin', with the jinx all around my bed.
Know I thought about you, an' honey, it liked to* kill me dead.

Oh, looka here now, baby, what you want me, what you want me, me to do?
Looka here honey, I say, what do you want poor me to do?
You know that I done all I could, just tryin' to get along with you.

You know, the blues ain't nothin' but a low-down shakin', low-down shakin', achin' chill.†
I say the blues is a low-down, old, achin' chill.
Well, if you ain't had 'em, honey, I hope you never will.

Well, the blues, the blues is a worried heart, is a worried heart, heart disease.
Oh, the blues is a worried old heart disease.
Look like the woman you be lovin', man, is so doggone hard to please.

I'd rather be outdoors, walkin' up, walkin' up and down the road.
I say, I'd rather be outdoors, I say, just walkin' up and down the road,
Than to be layin' around here, workin' just for my board and clothes.

Hey, looka here, little girl, don't you cry, don't you cry, cry no more.
I say, lookey here, darlin', honey, don't you try to cry no more.
Well, when I leave this time (*spoken:* I'm gonna) hang crepe on your door.

*The construction "like to," an equivalent of "likely to," was once standard English and
 appears in several blues.
†The comparison is probably to malaria.

Snatch It And Grab It *

Buddy Boy Hawkins

*To make the lyrics scan easier, we have omitted the spoken asides
by Hawkins and by Charlie Patton; who was present in the studio
when this song was recorded.

I bought my gal a hobble skirt,† boy, she's
    dressed up like a black crow bird,
Now, every time me an' her stomp out, boy,
    her shoes slide down in the mud.
I said, "Lookey here, black gal, now,
    don't you get 'smart'!"
She better stop to walkin' 'round me
    dressed so high‡
'Cause it ain't but one thing I'm gonna do,
    I'm gonna carry my hobble skirt!

Chorus:
I'm gonna snatch it, grab it, any way I can
    get it.
I'm gonna carry it back to be restored.
For now you know, gals, and I'm your pals',**
I haves all kind of a dough.
Now, all you womens dressin' up here look at me,
Now, you ain't got a pair of shoes at your feet!
I'm gonna snatch it, grab it, any way I can
    get it,
I'm gonna carry it back to be restored, I mean,
Take it back to be restored.

I'm gonna snatch it, grab it, any way I can
    get it.
I'm gonna take it back to be restored.
Well, you know gals, I'm your pals',
I haves all kind of a dough.
Now, all you womens dressin' up, look at me,
Now, you ain't got a pair of shoes at your feet!
I'm gonna snatch it . . . I'm gonna carry it back
    to be restored, I say,
I'm gonna carry it back to be restored.

I'm gonna grab it, any way I can get it,
Gonna take it back to be restored.
For you know, gals, and I'm your pals',
I haves all kind of a dough.
Now, all you women dressin' up, look at me,
Now, she ain't got a pair of shoes at her feet!
I'm gonna snatch it, grab it, I'm gonna
    take it back to be restored.

(Chorus of scat singing)

†Hobble skirts were in fashion around the turn of the century.
‡By "high" Hawkins probably means "high-toned"; he may use
"smart" in the previous line in the sense of stylish.
**We have placed an apostrophe after "pals" in the belief that
Hawkins intends to say "palsie"; otherwise, he has simply
blundered in pluralizing the word.

Alabama Blues

Robert Wilkins
Copyright © 1968 Wynwood Music Co. Inc.
All Rights Reserved   Used by Permission

I'll tell you, girl, I'm gonna tell you now,
If you don't want me, please don't dog me around,
If you don't want me, don't dog me around.

My home ain't here, it's in most any old town,
My home ain't here, it's in most any old town,
My home ain't here, it's most any old town.

I'm goin' up on a mountain and look down on the sea,
Saw a bullyin'* alligator, she was doin' that shivaree,
Saw a bullyin' alligator doin' the shivaree.

Tell me, friend, ever since that bullyin' *Stack* been made,
Kansas City, Missouri, has been her regular trade,
Kansas City, Missouri, been her regular trade.

The *Kate*'s† in the bend, the *Stack* is turnin' around and 'round,
The stern wheel knockin', friend, I'm Alabama bound,
The stern wheel knockin', I'm Alabama bound.

My mama told me, an' papa told me, too,
Said, "Brownskin women, son, gonna be the death of you."
Said, "Brownskin women gonna be the death of you."

I told mama last night, friends, and papa the night before,
"If brownskin women kill me, mama, let me go,"
"If brownskin women kill me, mama, let me go."

*bullyin': a once-fashionable superlative.
†Kate: The *Kate Adams*, a fabled Mississippi riverboat. The last of the
three boats bearing this name (all of which were operated by the James
Rees Duquesne Engine Works and all of which were destroyed by fire)
perished mysteriously in 1926, possibly at the hands of a bigot who
resented its appearance in the movie *Uncle Tom's Cabin.*

When I leave you that time, mama, I won't be back no more,
When I leave you that time, mama, I won't be back no more,
When I leave that time, mama, I won't be back no more.

I ain't comin' back here to worry you and papa so,
I won't be back here to worry you and papa so,
I won't be back here to worry you and papa so.

I walked off and left my mother standin' in the door,
She's cryin' to me, "Son, please son, don't you go,"
She's cryin' to me, "Son, please don't you go."

Texas Blues

Marshall Owens

I'm goin' back to Texas, hear the wild ox moan.

I'm goin' back to Tex-as, hear the wild ox moan.

Lord that's why, — you hear me — 'til— ear-ly morn.

I'm goin' back to Texas, hear the wild ox moan,
I'm goin' back to Texas, hear the wild ox moan,
Lord, that's why you hear me till early morn'.

Someday you gonna be sorry, honey, you done me wrong,
Someday, baby, honey, you done me wrong.
Honey, baby, all right, honey an' I'll be gone.

Third verse hummed.

Baby, baby, you don't know my mind,
Oh, baby, baby, you don't know my mind,
When you think I'm lovin' you, I'm leavin' all the time.

Lord, I woke up this mornin', baby, about the break of day,
I woke up this mornin', baby, at about the break of day,
I's huggin' the pillow where my fair brownie lay.

Sixth verse hummed.

My Creole Belle

Mississippi John Hurt

Medium slow

My Cre-ole belle,__ I love her well,__
my dar-lin' ba - by,__ My Cre-ole belle.__
When the stars__ shine,__ I'll call her mine,__
my dar-lin' ba - by,__ my Cre-ole belle.__

My Creole belle, I love her well,
My darlin' baby, my Creole belle.
When the stars shine I'll call her mine,
My darlin' baby, my Creole belle.

My Creole belle, I love her well,
I love her more anyone can tell.
My Creole belle, I love her well,
My darlin' baby, my Creole belle.

When the stars are shinin' I'll call her mine,
My darlin' baby . . .
My Creole belle, I love her well,
My darlin' baby, my Creole belle.

Sun Goin' Down

Son House

First verse hummed.

Well, you know the sun is goin' down, I say, behind that old western hill,
(On, on) . . . I say, behind that old western hill,
You know, I couldn't do a thing, not against my baby's will.

Man, you know that's bad, I declare that's too black bad,
. . . I declare that's too black bad,
You know, my woman done quit me, oh man, looks like the whole round world is glad.

You know, she stopped writin', wouldn't even send me no kinda word,
. . . I said she wouldn't send me no kinda word,
She turned her little old back on me 'bout some old low-down thing she heard.

Well, I'm goin' away, baby, I'm gonna stay a very long time,
I say, I'm gonna stay a great long time,
You know, I'm comin' back not un—whooh, baby—until you change your mind.

I wake up every mornin' feelin' sick and bad,
I said, soon every mornin' I be's feelin' sick and bad,
Thinkin' about the old time, baby, that I once have had.

If I don't go crazy, I say, I'm gonna lose my mind,
I believe I'm gonna lose my mind,
'Cause I stay worried—whooh, baby—all the, well, all the time.

Lookey here, baby, sit right chere on my knee,
I said, sit right down on my knee,
Well, I just wanna tell you just how you been doin' me.

What do you want poor me to do?
I say, whooh, what do you want me to do?
I been doin' all I can, honey, just tryin' to get along with you.

Final verse hummed.

Casey Jones*

Mississippi John Hurt
Copyright © 1963 Wynwood Music Co. Inc.
All Rights Reserved   Used by Permission

Medium

Cas - ey Jones___ was a brave en - gi - neer,___ he told

his fire - man to not to___ fear. (Says:)

"All I want, my wa - ter and my coal.

Look out the win - dow, see my drive - wheel___ roll."

Casey Jones was a brave engineer,
He told his fireman to not to fear.
Says, "All I want, my water and my coal.
Look out the window, see my drive wheel roll."

Early one mornin' came a shower of rain,
'Round the curve I seen a passenger train.
In the cabin was Casey Jones,
He's a noble engineerman but he's dead and gone.

"Children, children, get your hat."
"Mama, mama, what you mean by that?"
"Get your hat, put it on your head,
Go down in town, see if your daddy's dead."

"Mama, mama, how can it be?
My daddy got killed on the old I. C."†
"Hush your mouth and hold your breath,
You're gonna draw a pension after your
    daddy's dead."

Casey's wife, she got the news,
She was sittin' on the bedside, she was
    lacin' up her shoes.
I said, "Go away, children, and hold your breath,
You're gonna draw a pension after your
    daddy's dead."

Casey said, before he died,
"Fixed the blinds so the bums can't ride.
If they ride, let 'em ride the rod,
Trust they lives in the hands of God."

Casey said again, before he died,
One more road that he wanted to ride.
People wondered what road could that be?
The Gulf Colorado and the Santa Fe.

Casey Jones was a noble engineer,
He told his fireman to not, to not to fear.
Says, "All I want, my water and my coal,
Look out the window, see my drive wheel roll."

*According to folklorists, the real-life Jones crashed to death in
1900 en route to Canton, Mississippi. Nine years later, the famous
ballad (to which this version is musically unrelated) became a pop
hit; its legacy is a Casey Jones museum in Tennessee. Perhaps a
duller hero was never more celebrated in song.
†I. C.: Illinois Central line.

Voice Throwin' Blues*

Moderate

Buddy Boy Hawkins

Come in here and don't stay out late.__ If I call you__ don't you hes - i - tate.__ Tell me how long__ does I have to wait?__ Can I get you now__ (or must I hes - i - tate?__ __ Yeah, yeah, yeah, yeah. __

Come in here and don't stay out late,
If I call you, don't you hesitate.
Tell me, how long does I have to wait?
Can I get you now (or must I hesitate?
    Yea-yeah-yeah-yeah).

I ain't no miller, (no miller's son),
Can be your miller, your (miller comes.
    Listen here, how long)
Will I have to wait?
Can I get you now (or must I hesitate?
    Yea-yeah-yeah-yeah).

I might sing this verse, (it ain't nothin' new),
Makes me mad the . . .†
(Listen here, how long) will I have to wait?
Can I get you now, (or must I hesitate?)

Think yellow evil, (brownskin is, too),
Believe me, fair brown, I (don't need you.
    Listen here, how long)
Will I have to wait?
Can I get you now (or must I hesitate?)

Sayin', come in here and don't (stay out late),
If I call you don't (hesitate. Listen here,
    how long)
Will I have to wait?
Can I get you now (or must I hesitate?)

Mama told me, (daddy told me, too),
"Womens 'round here gonna be the (death of you."
    Listen here, how long)
Will I have to wait?
Can I get you now, (or must I hesitate?)

I ain't no doctor, (doctor's son),
Ease your pain till your (doctor comes.
    Listen here, how long)
Will I have to wait?
Can I get you now (or must I hesitate?)
Tell me, how long will I have to wait?
Can I get you now (or must I hesitate?
    Yea-yeah-yeah-yeah).

I don't want no sugar in my tea,
The woman I got sweet enough for me.
Baby, (how long) will I have to wait?
Can I get you now (or must I hesitate?
    Yea-yeah-yeah-yeah, unh huh).

*The parenthetical phrases in these verses indicate where Hawkins creates a comic effect by ventriloquy, delivering the punch lines conversationally in an exaggerated nasal voice. Except when he begins the line "Listen here, how long" in this fashion, this device does not disrupt the normal timing of the verses.
†Words inaudible.

You Don't Know My Mind

Joe Callicott
Copyright © 1969 Uncle Doris Music, Ltd. (United Kingdom)
65 Parkway, London, N.W.1 7PP.—U.S.A. controlled by
Uncle Doris Music, Inc. 165 West 74th Street, New York 10023
All Rights Reserved   Used by Permission

Medium fast

I'm a long time   long ways from home.—   Got no-bod-y (to lis-ten)

hear— me groan. Say   you don't   know,—   you don't   know   my mind.—

Aw, when you   see me   laugh-in',   I'm laugh-in'   to keep from . . . (cryin').

Spoken:
Good and plain.

I'm a long time, long ways from home,
Got nobody to listen, hear me groan.
Say, you don't know, you don't know my mind,
Aw, when you see me laughin', I'm laughin' to keep from . . .

What did the little red rooster told the hen?
"Pull your comb, won't ya, woman, snatch it again?"
Say, you don't know, you don't know my . . .
(*Spoken:* Bound to go!)
Aw, when you see me laughin', laughin' to keep from . . .

Well, told my baby just 'fore day,
"Can't do better, baby, says, I hate your way."
Say, you don't know, you don't know my mind,
Well, if you get in trouble, I'm bound to buy your fine.

Well now, you don't know, you don't know, you don't know my fractious* mind,
Baby, you don't know, you don't know my . . .
Aw, when you see me laughin', I'm laughin' to keep from cryin'.

Well, my baby got somethin', try to keep it hid,
Good Lord, give me somethin', well, to find it with.
Say, you don't know, you don't know my mind,
Aw, when you see me laughin', I'm laughin' just to keep from cryin'.

Say, if your woman happened to quit you, don't you take her back,
Get you a black gal, she'll come easin' back.
Say, you don't know, you don't know my . . .
Aw, when you see me laughin', I'm laughin' to keep from cryin'.

Well, it's somethin' here, now, that worryin' my mind,
Thinkin' about the little woman all the time.
Lord, you don't know, no, you don't know my . . .
Aw, when you see me laughin', I'm laughin' just keep from cryin'.

Well, I done got old, voice got low,
I don't wanna hang around your house no more.
Babe, say you don't know, you don't know my mind,
Aw, when you see me laughin', I'm laughin' to keep from cryin'.

Well, you don't know (*spoken:* Whup it again!), you don't know my doggone mind,
Baby, you don't . . . you don't know my . . .
Aw, when you see me laughin', I'm laughin' just keep from cryin'.

Well, I stood in New Jersey, walked over in New York town,
I didn't have a dime, had to turn around.
Say, you don't know, you don't know my mind,
Aw, when you see me laughin', I'm laughin' to keep from cryin'.

Down in old Hernando, Nesbitt town,†
In Mississippi, says, I got turned around.
Say, you don't know, you don't know my mind,
Aw, when you see me laughin', I'm laughin' just to keep from cryin'.

fractious: fretful
†The late Callicott hailed from the Hernando-Nesbitt area, which is just south
  of Memphis.

Hellhound On My Trail

Robert Johnson

I've got to keep movin', I've got to keep movin',
Blues fallin' down like hail, blues fallin' down like hail,
. . . blues fallin' down like hail, blues fallin' down like hail.
An' the days keeps on worryin' me, there's a hellhound on my trail,
Hellhound on my trail, hellhound on my trail.

If the day was Christmas eve, if the day was Christmas eve,
And the morrow was Christmas day,
If today was Christmas eve an' the morrow was Christmas day,
(*Spoken:* Aw, wouldn't we have a time, baby?)
I would need my little sweet rider just to pass the time away,
Uh huh, to pass the time away.

You sprinkle hot-foot powder all around my door, all around my door,
You sprinkle hot-foot powder all 'round your daddy's door,
It keep me with a ramblin' mind rider
Every old place I go, every old place I go.

I can tell the wind is risin',
The leaves tremblin' on the tree, tremblin' on the tree,
I can tell the wind is risin', leaves tremblin' on the tree.
All I need, my little sweet woman, an' to keep my company,
Hey-hey-hey-hey, my company.

Special Rider Blues

Skip James
Copyright © 1969 Wynwood Music Co. Inc.
All Rights Reserved   Used by Permission

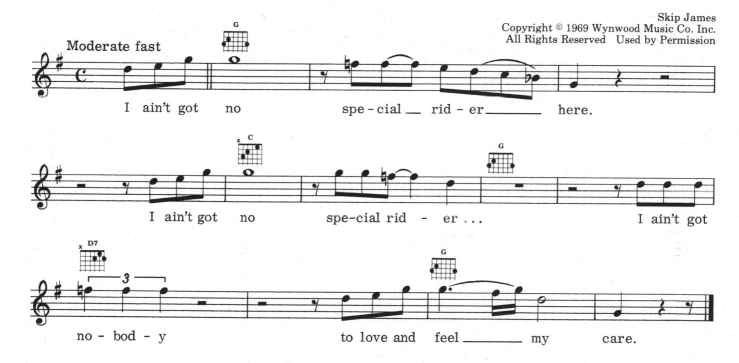

I ain't got no special rider here,*
I ain't got no special rider . . .
I ain't got nobody to love and feel my care.

I woke up this mornin', looked at the special risin' sun,
Got up this mornin', looked at special risin' sun,
An' I prayed to the Lord my special rider would go.

I sing this song to ease your trouble in mind,
Sing this song, ease your trouble in mind,
And you stay worried, yeah, and bothered all the time.

Hey, hey, what more can I do?
Hey, hey, what more can I do?
Honey, you must want me keep singin' these special blues.

*James understood the phrase "special rider" to mean a favorite
girl friend.

Get Away Blues

Robert Wilkins
Copyright © 1968 Wynwood Music Co. Inc.
All Rights Reserved   Used by Permission

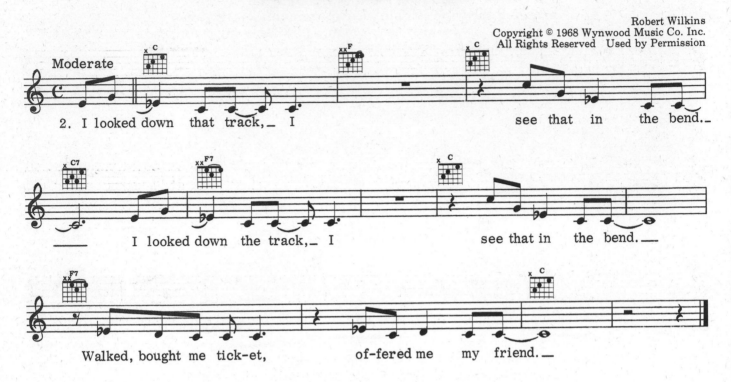

I walked down to the station, fold my troubled arms, (twice)
Walked and asked that agent, "Has that train been gone?"

I looked down that track, I see that in the bend, (twice)
Walked . . . bought me ticket, offered me my friend.

Told her, "Come on, woman, let us board this train, (twice)
Ride her while we get away from your man."

Woman, you just tell me, do you want to go? (twice)
I'll take you somewhere you never been before.

Then I'll give you silver, give you paper and gold, (twice)
I'll give you anything'll satisfy your worried soul.

Woman, if I don't love you, I don't love myself, (twice)
You did something to me I ain't gonna tell nobody else.

Bird Nest Bound

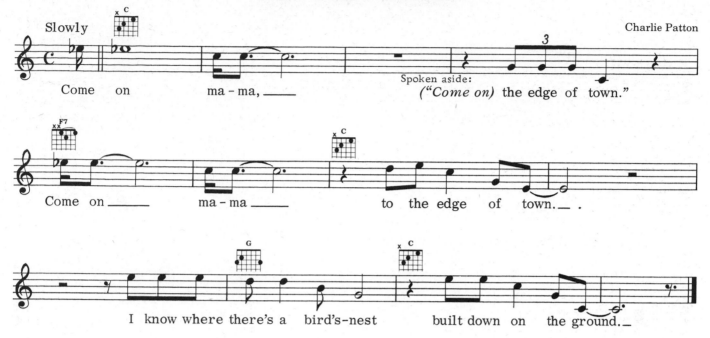

Slowly

Charlie Patton

Come on ma-ma, _____ *("Come on)* the edge of town."

Spoken aside:

Come on _____ ma-ma _____ to the edge of town._.

I know where there's a bird's-nest built down on the ground._

Come on, mama, *(spoken:* Come to) the edge of town,
Come on, mama, to the edge of town,
I know where there's a bird's nest, built down on the ground.

If I was a bird, mama . . .
If I was a bird, mama, I would, I'd nest in the heart of town,
(Spoken: Lord, you know I'd live in the heart of town)
So when the town get lonesome I'd be bird nest bound.

Hard luck is at your front door, blues are in your room,
Hard luck is at your front door, blues are in your room,
Callin' at your back door, "What is gonna become of you?"

Sometime I say I need you, then again I don't,
Sometime I say I need you, then again I don't,
(Spoken: You know it's the truth, baby)
Sometime I think I'll quit you, then again I won't.

Oh, I remember one mornin', stand in my baby's door,
(Spoken: Sure boy, I was standin' there)
Oh, I remember one mornin', stand in my baby's door,
(Spoken: Boy, you know what she told me?)
"Looka here, papa Charlie, I don't want you no more."

Safe sweet home, sweet home baby, through that shiny star,
Safe sweet home now through, aw, that shiny star,
You don't need no tellin', mama, I will take you in my car.*

*This line is preceded by an unintelligible vocal aside.

Big Leg Blues

Mississippi John Hurt
Copyright © 1964 Wynwood Music Co. Inc.
All Rights Reserved   Used by Permission

Raise up, baby, get your big leg offa mine,
Raise up, baby, get your big leg offa mine,
They're so heavy, make a good man change his mind.

I asked you, baby, to come and hold my head,
I ask you, baby, to come and hold my head,
Send me word that you'd rather see me dead.

I'm goin', I'm goin', your cryin' won't make me stay,
I'm goin', I'm goin', cryin' won't make me stay,
More you cry, the further you drive me away.

Some crave high yellow, I like black and brown,
Some crave high yellow, I like black and brown,
Black won't quit you, brown won't lay you down.

It was late at midnight and the moon shine bright like day,
It was late at midnight and moon shines bright like day,
I seen your faror* goin' up the right of way.

*The spelling of "faror," a Mississippi blues synonym for girl friend,
is problematic. It is pronounced like "pharaoh." The late Johnnie
Temple provided blues researcher Gayle Wardlow with the spelling
used.

Beer Drinkin' Women

B.K. Turner

Now if you got a jake-drink-ing wom-an, bud-dy, she don't mean you no good. If you got a beer-drink-ing wom-an, bud-dy, she don't mean you no good. She won't wash and iron your clo', won't e-ven love you like she should.

Now, if you got a jake-drinkin'* woman, buddy, she don't mean you no good,
If you got a beer-drinkin' woman, buddy, she don't mean you no good,
She won't wash and iron your clo', won't even love you like she should.

She will go to some fast place, buddy, and stay there all night long,
She will go to some fast place, buddy, and stay there all night long,
She'll tell you the next mornin', "Daddy, I'll never do you wrong."

Beer-drinkin' woman ain't no good, she don't even love herself,
Beer-drinkin' woman ain't no good, she don't even love herself,
And you oughta know by that, she don't love nobody else.

Now, if you got a beer-drinkin' woman, buddy, you better let her go,
If you got a beer-drinkin' woman, buddy, you better let her go,
'Cause if she don't send you to prison, she'll send you to the bone yard,† don't you know?

*jake: denatured alcohol. A toxic substance much worthier of the sordid woman Ace portrays
 than mere beer. (Perhaps derived from juke: African origin, Gullah, meaning disorderly or
 wicked.)
†bone yard: cemetery

Big Chief Blues

Traditional, Arranged by Furry Lewis
Copyright © 1969 Uncle Doris Music, Ltd. (United Kingdom)
65 Parkway, London, N.W.1 7PP.—U.S.A. controlled by
Uncle Doris Music, Inc. 165 West 74th Street, New York 10023
All Rights Reserved   Used by Permission

Baby, I'm so blue this mornin', Lord, I'm just as blue as bluin',*
So blue this mornin', baby, I'm just as blue as bluin'.
Woman I love is, well, she drivin' me to ruin.

I'm gonna marry, marry an Indian squaw,
Lord knows I'm gonna marry, I'm gonna marry an Indian squaw.
So the big chief can be Furry's daddy-in-law.

Well, I know my woman, she don't know I'm here,
If she do, she don't feel my care.
Boy, I know my . . . she sure don't know I'm here
Cryin', if she do, well, she do not feel my care.

I went to the gypsy for to get my hambone done,
I went to the gypsy for to get my hambone done.
Lord, the gypsy told me, "Furry, I 'clare you sure need one."

My Mondays' woman live on Beale and Main,
    and my Tuesdays' bring me pocket change.
Say my Mondays' woman, she live on Beale and Main,
Says my Tuesdays' woman will bring me pocket change.

*bluing: a substance, as indigo, used to whiten clothes or give them a
  bluish tinge.

Say, your hair ain't curly, says, and your eyes ain't blue,
Say, your hair ain't curly and your eyes ain't blue.
Say, there something, baby, says, is wrong with you.

Well, my Wednesdays' woman bring me daily news,
Well, my Wednesdays' woman bring me daily news.
Said my Thursdays' woman, well, she buy my socks and shoes.

Lord, my Fridays' woman, she puts it on the shelf,
Said, my Friday woman, she puts it all on the shelf.
My Saturday woman give me the devil if she ever catch me here.

Said my Sundays' woman cooks me somethin' to eat,
Make me have a woman for every day in the week.
Boys, I got a woman for every day in the week,
I got a woman for every day in the week.

I got a new way o' spellin' "Memphis, Tennessee"—
Double "m," double "e," great God, "a-y" and a "z."
I got a new way of spellin' "Memphis, Tennessee"—
Double "m," double "e," great God, "a-y" and a "z."

If you ever wanna hear me blow my lonesome horn,
Come to, to my number, boy, when my baby gone.
Boy, you wanna hear me blow my lonesome horn?
Come to my number, oh, when my baby gone.

I got a girl in Cubie an' got a girl in Spain,
Girl in Memphis, scared to call her name.
I got a girl in Cubie and got a girl in Spain,
I got a girl in Memphis, but I'm scared to call her name.

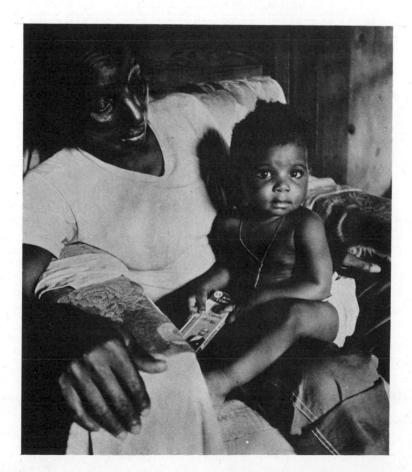

If I Had Possession Over My Judgment Day

Robert Johnson

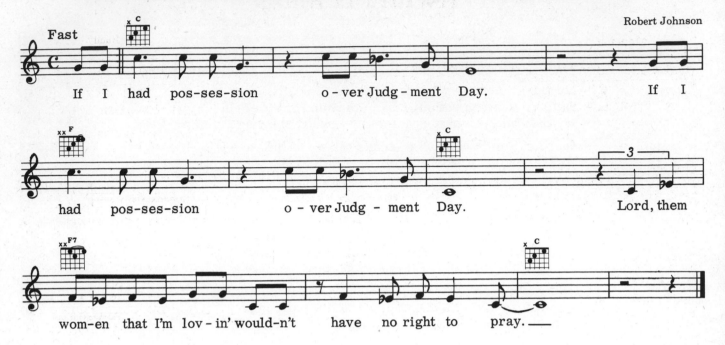

If I had possession over Judgment Day,
If I had possession over Judgment Day,
Lord, them women that I'm lovin' wouldn't have no right to pray.

An' I went to the mountain, looked as far as my eyes could see,
An' I went to the mountain, looked as far as my eye will see,
Some other man got my woman, an' these lonesome blues got me.

An' I rolled an' I tumbled an' I cried the whole night long,
An' I rolled an' I tumbled an' I cried the whole night long,
Boy, I woke up this mornin', my biscuit roller gone.

Had to fold my arms, an' I slowly walked away,
(*Spoken:* I didn't like the way she'd *done!*)
Had to fold my arms, an' I slowly walked away,
I felt in my mind your trouble gonna come someday.

Now, run here, baby, set down on my knee,
Now, run here, baby, set down on my knee,
I wanna tell you all about the way they've treated me.

Awful Fix Blues

Buddy Boy Hawkins

'Cause I'm a strang-er here wom-an, I just blowed in your,
I just blowed in your mam-lish town. I'm a strang-er to you, brown-skin
ma-ma, just blowed in your town.___ Says if I
ask you for a fa-vor, ma-ma, please ma'am don't turn me down.

Hey, mama, tell me what have I, tell me what have I—'tain't no lie!
Hey, mama, tell me what have I done?
Because seem like you're tryin'-a ease your lovin' fair brown down.

You're gonna wake up one of these mornings now, sweet mama, and I'll be,
Baby, mama, and I'll be—'tain't no lie, tell the truth!
You're gonna wake up one of these mornings, mama, say then I'll be gone.
And you may not never, mama, see me in your town no more.

'Cause I'm a stranger here, woman, I just blowed in your,
I just blowed in your mamlish town.
I'm a stranger to you, brownskin mama, just blowed in your town.
Says, if I ask you for a favor, mama, please ma'am, don't turn me down.

If you get one old woman, boy, you better get you five or,
You'd better get you five or—I mean six!
If you get one old woman, you'd better get you five or six.
So if that one happen to quit you, it won't leave you in no awful fix.

When I had you, pretty mama, you know I was tryin' to do the best I—
I mean could! Baby, it wasn't no lie!
I say when I had you, little black woman, I was tryin' to do the best I could.
Now your little daddy is gone, now who you gonna get to chop your wood?

Avalon Blues*

Mississippi John Hurt

Got to New York this mornin', just about half-past nine, (twice)
Hollerin' one mornin' in Avalon, couldn't hardly keep from cryin'.

Avalon is my hometown, always on my mind, (twice)
Pretty mamas in Avalon want me there all the time.

When the train left Avalon, throwin' kisses and wavin' at me, (twice)
Says, "Come back, daddy, and stay right here with me."

Avalon's a small town, have no great big range, (twice)
Pretty mamas in Avalon, they sure will spend your change.

New York's a good town, but it's not for mine, (twice)
Goin' back to Avalon, near where I have a pretty mama all the time.

*The occasion of this song was Hurt's 1928 visit to New York for an Okeh
  recording session.

Aberdeen Mississippi Blues*

Booker White
Copyright © 1969 Wynwood Music Co. Inc.
All Rights Reserved   Used By Permission

4. A - ber - deen is my home but the men don't want me a-round. A - ber - de - en is (my) home but mean men don't want me a-round. They know I'll take these wom - en and take them out of town.

I were over in Aberdeen, on my way to New Orleans,
I was over in the Aberdeen, on my way to New Orleans.
Them Aberdeen women told me they would buy my gasoline.

They's two little women that I ain't never seen,
They has two little women that I ain't never seen.
These two little women, they's from New Orleans.

I'm sittin' down in Aberdeen, with New Orleans on my mind,
I'm sittin' down in Aberdeen, with New Orleans on my mind.
But I believe them Aberdeen women is gonna make me lose my mind.

Aberdeen is my home, but they mens don't want me around,
Aberdeen is my home, but mean men don't want me around.
They know I'll take these women, and take them out of town.

Listen, you Aberdeen women, you know I ain't got no dime,
Listen, you women, you know I ain't got no dime.
They been, had the poor boy all hobbled down.

*White was raised in the vicinity of Aberdeen, and a post card sent to that
town ultimately resulted in his "rediscovery" several years ago.

My Black Mama

Son House

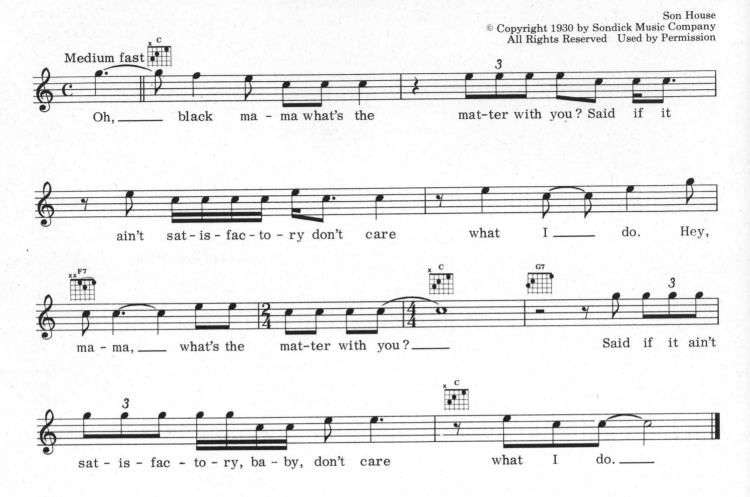

Oh, ___ black ma-ma what's the mat-ter with you? Said if it ain't sat-is-fac-to-ry don't care what I ___ do. Hey, ma-ma, ___ what's the mat-ter with you? ___ Said if it ain't sat-is-fac-to-ry, ba-by, don't care what I do. ___

Part One

Oh, black mama, what's the matter with you?
Said, if it ain't satisfactory, don't care what I do.
Hey, mama, what's the matter with you?
Said, if it ain't satisfactory, baby, don't care what I do.

You take a brownskin woman'll make a rabbit move to town,
Say, but a jet-black woman'll make a mule kick his stable down.
Oh, a brownskin woman will make a rabbit move to town,
Oh, but a real black woman'll make a mule kick his stable down.

Say, 'tain't no heaven, say, there ain't no burnin' hell,
Say, where I'm goin' when I die, can't nobody tell.
Oh, there ain't no heaven, now, there ain't no burnin' hell,
Oh, where I'm goin' when I die, can't nobody tell.

Well, my black mama's face shine like the sun,
Oh, lipstick and powder sure won't help her none.
My black mama's face shines like the sun,
Oh, lipstick and powder, well, they sure won't help her none.

Well, you see my milk cow, tell her to hurry home,
I ain't had no milk since that cow been gone.
If you see my milk cow, tell her to hurry home,
Yeah, I ain't had no milk since that cow been gone.

Well, I'm goin' to the racetrack to see my pony run,
He ain't the best in the world, but he's a runnin' son-of-a-gun.
I'm goin' to the racetrack to see my pony run,
He ain't the best in the world, but he's a runnin' son-of-a-gun.

Oh, Lord have mercy on my wicked soul,
Wouldn't mistreat you, baby, for my weight in gold.
Oh, Lord have mercy on my wicked soul,
(Last line hummed).

Part Two

Hey, I solemnly swear, Lord, I raise my right hand,
That I'm gonna get me a woman, you can get you another man.
I solemnly swear, Lord, I raise my right hand,
That I'm gonna get me a woman, babe, you get you another man.

I got a letter this mornin', how do you think it read?
"Oh, hurry, hurry, the gal you love is dead."
I got a letter this mornin', how do you reckon it read?
"Oh, hurry, hurry, the gal you love is dead."

I grabbed my suitcase, I took off up the road,
I got there, she was layin' on the coolin' board.
I grabbed my suitcase, I took on up the road,
Oh, when I got there, she was layin' on the coolin' board.

Well, I walked up close, I looked down in her face,
Good old gal, you got to lay here till Judgment Day.
I walked up close, and I looked down in her face,
Yes, been a good old gal, got to lay here till Judgment Day.

Spoken:
Aw sho' now, I feel low-down this evenin'!

Oh, my woman so black, she stays apart of this town,
Can't nothin' "go" when the poor gal is around.
My black mama stays apart of this town,
Oh, can't nothin' "go" when the poor gal is around.

Oh, some people tell me the worried blues ain't bad,
It's the worst old feelin' that I ever had.
Some people tell me the worried blues ain't bad,
Buddy, the worst old feelin', Lord, I ever had.

Mmm, I fold my arms, and I walked away,
"That's all right, mama, your trouble will come someday."
I fold my arms, Lord, I walked away,
Say, "That's all right, mama, your trouble will come someday."

Hot Jelly Roll Blues

George Carter

Jelly roll, jelly roll, you can see it on the fence,
If you don't go and get it, you ain't got no sense.

Chorus (repeat after each verse):
I'm wild 'bout my jelly, 'bout my jelly roll,
When you taste my jelly, (you) mamas change your glad home.

It make a blind man see, a lame man walk,
It make a deaf woman hear and a little baby talk.

Gonna tell all you people what jelly roll done done,
Made grandmama marry her younger grandson.

Jelly roll is a thing a man won't do without it,
He'll get plain unruly if the people put him out.

I went up on the mountain, looked down in the sea,
A good-lookin' woman winked her eye at me.

If you don't believe my jelly roll'll do,
You can ask anybody on Holman Avenue.

At Home Blues

Sam Hopkins
Copyright © 1971 Tradition Music Co.
All Rights Reserved   Used by Permission

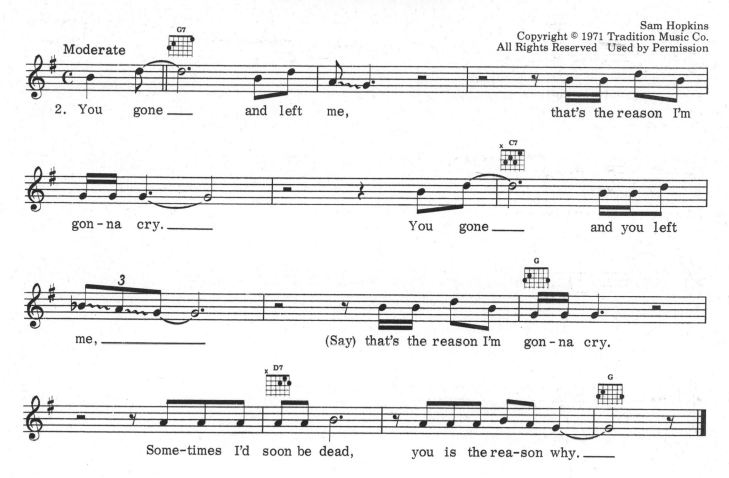

2. You gone ___ and left me, that's the reason I'm gon-na cry. ___ You gone ___ and you left me, ___ (Say) that's the reason I'm gon-na cry. Some-times I'd soon be dead, you is the rea-son why. ___

Spoken Introduction:
Yeah, when I was at home with mama, baby, she
wouldn't let me be. Now I made a song about you
women. I'm gonna tell you just how it goes—just
like this:

When I was at home with mama, you women wouldn't let me be,
When I was at home with you, mama, you women wouldn't let me be.
You know, that's the reason I'm 'way from home today.

You gone and left me, that's the reason I'm gonna cry,
You gone and you left me, say, that's the reason I'm gonna cry.
Sometimes I'd soon be dead, you is the reason why.

But if you ever see my brother, woman, please tell him for me,
See my brother, see my brother, woman, please tell him for me:
The reason I'm away from home, you women wouldn't let me be.

All Night Long

Skip James

If it's all night long, mama, if it's all night long,
If it's all night long, mama, Lord, if it's all night long.
If you ain't got no hay, mama, better be on your way,
You ain't got no hay, mama, Lord, you better be on your way.

Hitch on my pony, mama, saddle my black mare,
You'll find me ridin', mama, Lord, in the world somewhere.
In the world somewhere, in the world somewhere,
You'll find me ridin', mama, Lord, in the world somewhere.

If you haven't any hay, mama, let's go down the road,
If you haven't any hay, mama, let's go down the road.
If it's all night long, if it's all night long,
If it's all night long, mama, if it's all night long.

Get your bucket and your basket, let's go to the wood,
Don't find no berries, mama, Lord, got to make lovin' good.
If it's all night long, if it's all night long,
If it's all night long, mama, if it's all night long.

Make me one pallet, mama, make it on the floor,
Make it calm and easy, mama, Lord, so nobody'll never know, never . . .
Nobody'll never know, nobody'll never . . .
Make it calm and easy, mama, Lord, so nobody'll never . . .

Continue Refrain:
If it's all night long, if it's all night . . .
If it's all night long, if it's all night long.

Give me one key, mama, to your back door,
You'll never be bothered, baby, with me on the front no more.
Oh never, never—never, never no more,
You will never be bothered, baby, with me on the front no more.

If it's all night long, if it's all night . . .
If it's all night long, if it's all night long.

'Bout A Spoonful

Arranged by Mance Lipscomb
Copyright © 1970 Tradition Music Co.
All Right Reserved   Used By Permission

I've been drinkin' bad whiskey all night long, got the headache now,
Yes, I been drinkin' bad whiskey all night long, oh Lord, mama, got the headache now.

Tell me, what you gonna do with your brand-new daddy, 'bout a spoonful?
Tell me, what you gonna do with your brand-new papa, oh Lord, mama, 'bout a spoonful?

And late last night when come home from gettin' a spoonful,
It was late last night I come home from gettin' a spoonful.

Oh Lordie, mama, oh Lord, daddy, just a spoonful,
All I want, baby, in this world, oh baby, just a spoonful.

Eve and Adam was the first two people got a spoonful,
Tell me, Eve and Adam was the first two people, oh mama, got a spoonful.

Late last night when I lay down and got a spoon . . .
Baby, late last night I lay down, oh mama, got a spoonful.

Oh, I drinkin' bad whiskey all night long, got the headache now,
I been drinkin' bad whiskey all night long, oh mama, got the headache now.

Tell me, what you gonna do with your brand-new daddy, 'bout a spoonful?
Oh what you gonna do with your brand-new daddy, 'bout a spoonful?

Put him in the bed, gonna run him crazy, 'bout a spoonful,
Put him in the bed, gonna run him crazy, oh Lord, mama, 'bout a spoonful.

All I want in this wide world is just a spoonful,
Baby, all I want in this wide world is just a spoonful.

Tell me, what you gonna do with your brand-new mama, 'bout a spoonful?
Tell me, what you gonna do with your brand-new mama, oh Lord, baby, 'bout a spoonful?

Dough Roller Blues

Joe Callicott

Spoken:
Goin'. I'm goin' now.

I was down, I was down, have no way to do, (*spoken:* Doggone!)
I was down, I didn't have a dime.
Well, the woman I thought loved me didn't pay me no mind.

Well, I'm goin' away, worry any day,
I'm goin' away, try to be worried any . . .
Well, I love that woman an' her dirty way.

Well, then don't your (*spoken:* house feel lonesome), dough roller gone?
Don't your house feel lonesome, dough roller . . . ?
You ain't got nobody to carry your good rollin' on.

I'll cut your throat, woman, drink your blood like wine,
I'll cut your throat, woman, drink your blood like wine.
Well, I was crazy about the woman and she wasn't none of mine.*

If you steal my jelly, says I won't get mad with you,
If you steal my jelly roll, won't get mad with you.
Well, the day comin', steal someone else's too.

*I.e., she has another lover.

98

Spoken:
Play it now, play it . . . take your time . . . do it right.

Well, the rooster crowed 'fore day, says, and I got away,
Lord, Lord, Lord, and the rooster crow . . . day and I got away.
Well, I'm lovin' you baby and I hate your way.

Well, the way that you got caused a good man in his grave,
(*Spoken:* Don't wanna go there!)
Well, the way you got caused a good man in his . . .
I'm ragged and dirty, baby, don't drive me away.

Well, I hit my baby, I try to knock her down,
(*Spoken:* Look out there!)
Well, I hit my baby, says, I try to knock her down.
I was a poor boy rambling on the edge o' town.

Spoken:
Look out there! Gonna play some music now, look out!

Well now, just 'fore day, say, the blues creeped down on me,
Well now, just 'fore day, say, the blues creeped down on me.
Well, my heart in trouble, achin' in misery.

I'm a poor boy, great long ways from home, (*spoken:* Look out there!)
I'm a poor boy, great long ways from home.
I ain't got nobody to carry my good work on.

Spoken:
Get funny, now! Look here! Gettin' funny. . . .

Well, you take my woman, says I won't be get mad with you,
Double do love you baby. . . .

Well, you can't tell woman's on the line, Lord,†
Lord, you can't never tell when a woman's on the line.
Well, I don't go crazy, sure gonna lose my mind.

†This phrase is presumably related to "lined," an old idiom meaning married.

Hambone Blues

. . . Regardless to what you got that she wants, and regardless to how pretty you think she is, you'll love her just to a certain extent and she'll love you just to a certain extent. But she'll lie and pretend that she loves you more than that.

——Skip James

Ed Bell

Jel-ly roll, _____ jel-ly roll, jel-ly roll is so hard to _____ find._

_____ Ain't a bak-er in town can bake a sweet jel-ly roll like mine.

Jelly roll, jelly roll, jelly roll is so hard to find,
Ain't a baker in town can bake a sweet jelly roll like mine.

I got to go to Cincinnati, just to have my hambone boiled,
Womens in Alabama gon' get my hambone spoiled.

Well, she mine and she yours, and she's somebody else's, too,
Don't you mention about rollin', 'cause she'll play a trick on you.

That's the way, that's the way these barefooted soul'll do,
They will get your money and they'll have a man on you.

You come home at night, she got a towel on her head,
Don't you mention about rollin', 'cause she'll swear she's nearly dead.

Jelly roll, jelly roll, will you see what you went and done?
You done had my grandpa, now you tried his youngest son.

I'm gettin' tired of walkin', I believe I'll slide a while,
I'm gettin' tired of women tellin' me their lies.

I wanna know, what make grandpa, hey, love your grandma so?
She got the same jelly roll she had forty years ago.

Got The Blues, Can't Be Satisfied

Mississippi John Hurt
Copyright © 1964 Wynwood Music Co. Inc.
All Rights Reserved   Used by Permission

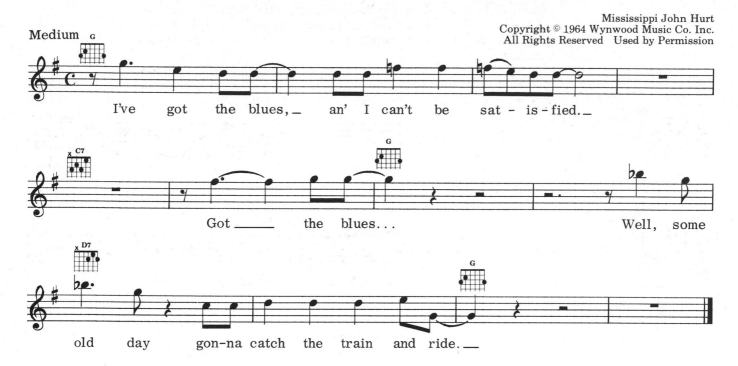

I've got the blues an' I can't be satisfied,
Got the blues . . .
Well, some old day, gonna catch the train
and ride.

Yes, whiskey straight will drive the blues away,
Whiskey straight will drive the blues away,
That be the case, I wants a quart today.

I bought my baby a great big diamond ring,
Bought my baby . . .
Come right back home and caught her
shakin' that thing.*

I said, "Babe, what make you do me this a-way?
Baby, what make you . . .
Well, that I bought, now you give it away."

I took my gun and I broke the barrel down,
Took my gun . . .
I put that joker six feet in the ground.

Yet got the blues and I still ain't satisfied,
You got the blues . . .
Well, some old day, gonna catch the train
and ride.

*shakin' that thing: blues euphemism for engaging in sex, popularized
by Papa Charlie Jackson's 1925 hit "Shake That Thing."

Future Blues

Willie Brown

Moderate

2. The min-utes seems like ho-urs an' ho-urs seems like days.

An' the min-utes seems like ho-urs an' ho-urs seems like days.

An' it seems like my wom an ought-a

stop her low-down way.

Can't tell my future, honey, I can't tell my past.
Lord, it seems like every minute sure gonna be my last.

The minutes seems like hours, an' hours seems like days,
An' the minutes seems like hours, hours seems like days.
An' it seems like my woman oughta stop her low-down way.

Lord, the woman I love, now, she's five feet from the ground,
I says, woman I love, mama, is five feet from the ground.
And she's tailor-made and ain't no hand-me-down.

Lord, and I got a woman now, Lordie, she lightnin' when she,
    lightnin' when she, mamlish smiles.
I says, I've got a woman, Lord, she lightnin' when she smiles.
Five feet and four inches, and she's just good huggin' size.

Girl, I know, you see that picture now, Lordie, up, up on your mother's,
    up on your mother's, mama's shelf?
I know, you see that picture, Lord, up on your motherin' shelf?
Girl, you know by that I'm gettin' tired o' sleepin' by myself.

And it's "T" for Texas, now, and it's "T" for Tennessee,
And it's "T" for Texas, Lord, it's "T" for Tennessee.
Lord bless that woman that put the thing on me.

I'm So Glad

Skip James
Copyright © 1967 Wynwood Music Co. Inc.
All Rights Reserved   Used by Permission

Fast

(And) I'm so glad,— (and) I'm so glad,— I am glad,— I'm glad. I don't know what to do, don't know what to do; I don't know what— to do.— I'm tir - ed of weep-in', tired— of moan - in', — tired of groan-in' for you. —

And I'm so glad, and I am glad. I am glad, I'm glad.
I don't know what to do, don't know what to do. I don't know what to do.*
I'm tired of weepin', tired of moanin', tired of groanin' for you.

And I'm so glad, I am glad. I am glad, I'm glad.
I'm tired of weepin', tired of moanin', tired of groanin' for you.
And I'm so glad, and I am glad. I am glad, I'm glad.

I'm so tired of moanin', tired of groanin', tired of longin' for you.
I'm so glad, and I am glad. I am glad, I'm glad.
I don't know what to do, know what to do. I don't know what to do.
I'm so tired, and I am tired. I am tired . . .

And I'm so glad, I am glad. I am glad, I'm glad.
I don't know what to do, know what to do. I don't know what to do.
I'm tired of weepin', tired of moanin', tired of groanin' for you.
And I am so glad, and I am glad. I am glad, I'm glad.

I'm so tired, and I am tired. I am tired, I'm tired.
I'm tired of weepin', tired of moanin', tired of groanin' for you.
I'm so glad, and I am glad. I am glad, I'm glad.
I don't know what to do, know what to do. Don't know what to do.

*The seemingly illogical juxtaposition of "I'm so glad" and "I don't know
what to do" was likely a figure of black speech or song, inasmuch as Tarter
and Gay's "Brownie Blues" (1928) contains the phrase, "So glad I'm a
brownskin, I don't know what to do."

My Mother Died

My moth-er died and left me, boy, when I was only two years old.

My moth-er she died and left me, when I was on-ly two years old.

But I can re-mem-ber just as well, when I was crawl-in' from door to door.

Spoken Introduction:
My next selection will be, "My Mother Died and
Left Me When I Was Two Years Old."

My mother died and left me, boy, when I was only two years old,
My mother, she died and left me when I was only two years old.
But I can remember just as well when I was crawlin' from door to door.

That's the reason you hear the people say, "Motherless children have a hard, hard time,"
That's the reason you hear the people say, "Motherless children have a hard, hard time."
. . . I can remember when I was goin' from door to door.*

I was stayin' at a old lady, that old lady she was too sick to see about me,
I was stayin' with a old lady, that old lady she was too sick to see about me.
I was walkin' around here so hungry, I was goin' from door to door.

I was motherless and fatherless, I was sisterless and brotherless, too,
I was motherless and fatherless, I was sisterless and brotherless, too.
That old lady did the best that she could do, oh, but I would wake up, I would be out, out of door.†

*We are unable to decipher part of this verse.
†I.e., outdoors

104

I was my mother's baby, my mother she died and left me alone,
I was my mother's child, my mother she died and left me alone.
Just a little before my mother died, she called me and she looked me dead in my eyes,

She said, "Son, you just now beginnin' to be two years old,"
My mother said, "Son, you just beginnin' to 'come two years old."
My mother said, "Now I'm gonna die, and you gonna have a hard time comin' up in the world."

I remember a pillow upon my baby's dyin' bed,‡
I remember a pillow upside my mother's dyin' bed.
My mother was wavin' to tell the people to take me away,
     'cause she know I didn't know what was goin' on.

But since I been grown, I been grown, I have my mother's bed,
Since I growed up and I done got grown, I have my mother's dying bed.
I look on the pillow where my mother, where my mother cast her eyes and say good-bye.

Oooh whooh, little girl, here the bed . . .
Here's the bed, here the bed where my mother laid her head.
She said, "Son, if you grow up and get to growin', don't let a decent meal get away."

Spoken:
She went out now with the red light.

‡Though now archaic, "dying bed" was a common figure of nineteenth century speech, and Skip
 James's song expression "sick bed" may derive from it.

Special Rider Blues

Son House
Copyright © 1941 by Sondick Music Company
All Rights Reserved   Used by Permission

Medium fast

2. Well, look-y here_ hon', I won't be your dog no more._

Well, look-y here_ hon', I won't be your dog no more._

Ex-cuse me hon-ey for knock-ing on your door._

Well, I'm goin' away, honey, I won't be back no more,
Well, I'm goin' away, honey, I won't be back no more,
When I leave this time, I'm gonna hang crepe on your door.

Well, lookey here, hon', I won't be your dog no more,
Well, lookey here, hon', I won't be your dog no more,
Excuse me, honey, for knockin' on your door.

I say your hair ain't curly and your doggone eyes ain't blue,
You know your hair ain't curly and your doggone eyes ain't blue,
Well, if you don't want me, what the world I want with you?

Say, lookey here, baby, you ought not to dog me around,
I say lookey here, baby, you ought not to dog me around,
If I had my belongings I would leave this old bad-luck town.

You know that's a shame, what a low-down, dirty shame,
Don't you know that's a shame? What a low-down old dirty shame,
You know I'm sorry today that I ever knowed your name.

I'm Satisfied*

Medium slow

Mississippi John Hurt
© Copyright 1963 Olwen Music
All Rights Reserved   Used by Permission

I'm sat-is-fied, ___ tick-led too, ___ old e-nough to mar-ry you. ___ I'm sat-is-fied ___ it's gon-na bring you back. I'm sat-is-fied, ___ ___ tick-led too, ___ old e-nough to mar-ry you. ___ I'm sat-is-fied ___ it's gon-na bring you back. ___

Guitar Solo

I'm satisfied, tickled, too. Old enough to marry you.
I'm satisfied it's gonna bring you back.
I'm satisfied, tickled, too. Old enough to marry you.
I'm satisfied it's gonna bring you back.

First in the country, then in town. I'm a total old shaker from my navel on down.
I'm satisfied it's gonna bring you back.
I'm satisfied, tickled, too. Old enough to marry you.
I'm satisfied it's gonna bring you back.

I pull my dress to my knees, I give my total all to who I please.
I'm satisfied it's gonna bring you back.
I'm satisfied, tickled, too. Old enough to marry you.
I'm satisfied it's gonna bring you back.

I'm satisfied, tickled, too. Old enough to marry you.
I'm satisfied it's gonna bring you back.
I'm satisfied, tickled, too. Old enough to marry you.
I'm satisfied it's gonna bring you back.

*The "speaker" of this courtship song is obviously feminine.

You Don't Mean Me No Good

Mance Lipscomb
Copyright © 1970 Tradition Music Co.
All Rights Reserved   Used by Permission

Baby, you don't mean me no good nohow,
Baby, baby, you don't mean me no good nohow,
But I'm gonna let you go, baby, I don't need no woman now.

Got up one mornin', I sure was feelin' bad,
Got up one mornin', I sure was feelin' bad,
Thought about my baby and the only girl I had.

Everybody hollerin' "mercy!" Wonder what do "mercy" mean?
Everybody hollerin' "mercy!" Wonder what do "mercy" mean?
If it means any good, Lord have mercy on me.

I met a man this mornin', down on bended knee,
I met a man this mornin', down on bended knee,
Say, it wasn't for no religion, "Gimme my good gal, please."

"If you gimme my woman, Lord, I won't bother you no more,
If you gimme my woman, Lord, I won't bother you no more,
You put her in my house, just leave her at my door."*

If I feel tomorrow like I feel today,
Feel tomorrow like I feel today,
I'm gonna pack my clothes and make my getaway.

My baby she left, didn't even shake my hand,
My baby done left me, didn't even shake my hand,
That's all right, mama, some day you're gonna understand.

*In an effort to make his phrase scan easier, Lipscomb has apparently
truncated the punch line, which Blind Willie McTell delivers as,
"You ain't got to put her in my house, I'm gonna lead her to my
door," in his "Broke-Down Engine Blues."

Baby, baby, what's the matter with you?
Oh, baby, baby, what's the matter with you?
You just don't treat me like you used to do.

I'm goin' away, to wear you off my mind,
I'm goin' away, just to wear you off my mind,
'Cause you keeps me worryin', bothered all the time.

Hardtime Killing Floor Blues*

4. Well, you hear me sing-in' my (blue) lone-some song,— These hard times can last us so

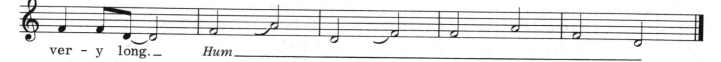

ver - y long.— Hum _____

Hard time here and everywhere you go,
Times is harder than ever been before.

And the people are driftin' from door to door,
Can't find no heaven, I don't care where they go.

Hear me tell you people, just before I go,
These hard times will kill you just dry long so.†

Well, you hear me singin' my (blue?) lonesome song,
These hard times can last us so very long.

If I ever get off this killin' floor,
I'll never get down this low no more.
No-no, no-no, I'll never get down this low no more.

And you say you had money, you better be sure,
'Cause these hard times will drive you from door to door.

Sing this song and I ain't gonna sing no more,
Sing this song and I ain't gonna sing no more.
. . . hard times will drive you from door to door.

*This is the title of the original Paramount recording (1931) of
James's topical Depression piece, which he called by the more
serviceable title, "Hard Times."
†dry long so: Pointlessly, without a cause.

Illinois Blues

Skip James
Copyright © 1968 Wynwood Music Co. Inc.
All Rights Reserved   Used by Permission

You go to Banglin',* tell my boys,
You go to Banglin', tell my boys
What times I'm havin' up in Illinois,
In Illinois, up in Illinois.

When I gin my little cotton I'm going to sell
    my seed,
When I gin my little cotton and sell my seed,
I'm gonna give my baby everything she need,
Everything she need, everything she need.
I'm gonna give my baby everything she need.

You know, I been in Texas and I been
    in Arkansas,
I been in Texas and I been in Arkansas,
But I never had a good time till I got to Illinois,
Up in Illinois, up in Illinois.

The people will treat you just so-so so',†
The people will treat you just so so',
You'll never go back to old Banglin' no more,
Never no more, never no more.

I been to Chicago and I been to Detroit,
I been to Chicago and I been to Detroit,
But I never had a good time till I got
    up in Illinois,
In Illinois, up in Illinois.

When you go down in Banglin', will you tell
    my boys?
When you go down in Banglin', tell my boys
What a good time's a-waitin' up in Illinois,
Up in Illinois, up in Illinois.

*"Banglin'" (James's spelling) was Skip James's own pet name
for a lumber camp operating out of Pelahatchie, Mississippi,
that employed him as a timber-cutter in the early twenties. His
explanation of this word coinage—that it followed from the camp's
"saggy" position on a bluff—suggests that it may have arisen
through confusion with "dangling."
†*so'*: soft

110

I'll Go With Her Blues

Robert Wilkins
Copyright © 1968 Wynwood Music Co. Inc.
All Rights Reserved   Used by Permission

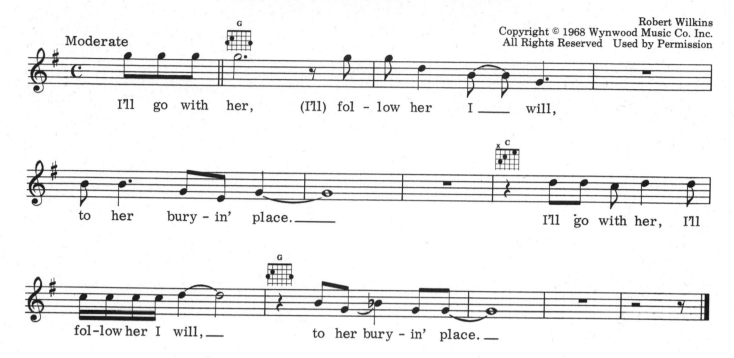

I'll go with her, I'll follow her, I will, to her buryin' place,
I'll go with her, I'll follow her, I will, to her buryin' place.

Hang my head and cry, friend, I will, as she passed away,
Hang my head and cry, friend, I will, as she passed away.

I thought I should go, friend, please run, try to call her back,
I thought I should go, friend, please run, tried to call her back.

'Cause that sure is one woman I did love and like,
For that sure is one woman I did, I did love and like.

I believe I'll go home, friend, and duly dress myself in black,
I believe I'll go home, friend, and duly dress myself in black.

Show to the world I wants her, but I can't get her back,
Show to the world I wants her, but I can't, I can't get her back.

Every time I hear that lonesome church bell ring,
Every time I hear that lonesome church bell ring,

It makes me think about that song my baby used to sing,
It makes me think about that song my baby used to sing.

Lord have mercy on me. . . .

Furry's Blues (No. 2)

Furry Lewis

Babe, I know you don't want me, you ain't got to dog me 'round,
Babe, I know you don't want me, you ain't got to dog me 'round.
(*Spoken:* Yes, girl, I told her!)
Oh, gimme my clothes, well Lord, I will shake 'em on down.

Oh, my baby says she didn't want me no more,
But she's on my dangle everywhere I go.
Say, my baby didn't want me no more,
Well, she's on my dangle, well, everywhere I go.

Spoken:
Hey you-all, just listen!

Someday you're gonna want me and I 'clare an' I won't want you,
Someday you may want me, babe, and I 'clare and I won't want you.
That'll be all right with me babe, just any old way you do.

Spoken:
You ever see anybody play a guitar with their elbow? Watch.

Well, I know you don't want me, why don't you tell me so?
Baby won't be bothered with . . . 'round your house no more.
Babe, I know you don't . . . why don't you tell me so?
(*Spoken:* Here's what's called the 'Eagle Rock' "*)
Well, you won't be bothered with Furry 'round your house no more.

Oh, big leg lady, take your big leg offa me,
Whoah, big leg lady, take your big leg offa me.
Baby, I ain't so tired but I'm just as sleepy as I can be.

Well, my mama dead, my papa across the sea,
Got nobody speak n'ar a good word for me.
My mama . . . papa 'cross the sea, (*spoken:* Yeah!)
I ain't got nobody, whoah, to love and care for me.

You can scold me here but you can't when I go home,
I got somethin' at home will make you let Furry alone.†
I got somethin' at home will make you let me alone,
Oh baby, will make you let me alone.

*In other words, the accompaniment will lend itself to dancing the
Eagle Rock.
†According to the late Skip James, the "something" of this traditional
verse is a pistol.

Ramblin' On My Mind

Robert Johnson

I've got ramblin', I've got ramblin' on my mind, ___
I've got ramblin', I've got ramblin' all on my mind.
Hate to leave my ba-by, ___ but you treats me so un-kind.

I've got ramblin', I've got ramblin' on my mind,
I've got ramblin', I've got ramblin' all on my mind,
Hate to leave my baby, but you treats me so unkind.

I got mean things, I got mean things all on my mind,
Little girl, little girl, I got mean things all on my mind,
Hate to leave you here, babe, but you treats me so unkind.

Runnin' down to the station, catch the first mail train I see,
(*Spoken:* I think I hear her comin' now)
Runnin' down to the station, catch that old first mail train I see.
I've got the blues 'bout Miss so-an'-so,
    an' the child has got the blues 'bout me.

An' I'm leavin' this mornin', with my arms fold up an' cryin',
An' I'm leavin' this mornin', with my arms fold up an' cryin',
I hate to leave my baby, but she treats me so unkind.

I got mean things, I've got mean things on my mind,
I got mean things, I got mean things all on my mind,
I got to leave my baby, for she treats me so unkind.

Get On Down The Road

Skip James
Copyright © 1969 Wynwood Music Co. Inc.
All Rights Reserved   Used by Permission

If you haven't any hay, get on down the road,
If you haven't any hay, mama Lord, go, get on down the road.
Get on down the road,
Get on down the road.
If you haven't any hay, mama, Lord, go, get on down the road.

I'm goin', I'm goin', comin' here no more,
If I go to Louisiana, mama Lord, though, they'll hang me sure.
They'll hang me sure,
They'll hang me sure.
If I go to Louisiana, mama Lord, they hang me . . .

If you haven't any hay, get on down the road,
If you haven't any hay, Lord, Lord, get on down the road.

I'm goin', I'm goin', comin' back no more,
I'm goin', I'm goin', partner, never comin' back no more,
Comin' back no more,
Comin' back no . . .
I'm goin', I'm goin', mama, never comin' back no . . .

Hey hey, hey-hey-hey-hey,
Hey-hey-hey-hey-hey-hey-hey,
Hey hey hey hey . . .

Hitch up my buggy, saddle up my black mare,
You'll find me a rider, mama, Lord, so in this world somewhere.
In this world somewhere,
In this world somewhere.
You can find me a rider, mama, look here, in this world somewhere.

If you haven't any hay, get on down the road,
If you haven't any hay, mama, look here, get on down the . . .
Get on down the road,
Get on down the road.
If you haven't any hay, mama, look here, get on down the . . .

If You Don't Want Me

Mississippi John Hurt
Copyright © 1964 Wynwood Music Co. Inc.
All Rights Reserved   Used by Permission

Moderately slow

4. Don't want me ba-by, got to have me any-how.

Don't want me ba-by, got to have me any-how.

Guitar interlude (length varies)   It was late

last night when ev-'ry - thing was still.   *Guitar interlude (length varies)*

If you don't want me, baby, got to have me anyhow,
If you don't want me, baby, got to have me anyhow.

It was late last night when everything was still,
Well, me and your baby eased out on the hill.

I tried my best to do my father's will,
I tried my best to do my father's will.

Don't want me, baby, got to have me anyhow,
Don't want me, baby, got to have me anyhow.

The sun go down, ain't this a lonesome place?
The sun goin' down and ain't this a lonesome place?

So lonesome here, can't see in my baby's face,
It's so lonesome here, I can't see in my baby's face.

You don't want me, baby, got to have me anyhow,
Don't want me, baby, got to have me anyhow.

How Long Buck*

Skip James
Copyright © 1965 Wynwood Music Co. Inc.
All Rights Reserved   Used by Permission

How long, ___ how long, has my crow_ Jane treat me wrong?

So long (baby), so long, ba-by, so long. I got_

How long, how long has my crow jane treat
  me wrong?
So long, (baby) so long, baby, so long.

I got to the station, she left town,
I'm blue and disgusted and nobody been down,
But hey, so long, baby, so long, baby, so long.

How long, how long has my crow jane been
  so wrong?
So long, so long, baby, so long.

I could holler like a jack,†
I'd go to the mountain, call her back,
How long, baby, how long, baby, how . . . ?

How long, been so long, am I to be
  treated wrong?
How long, how long, baby, how long?

I got to the station, she left town,
I couldn't hardly change her mind,
How long, how long, baby, how long?

Aw, someday you'll be sorry you treated
  me wrong,
It'll be too late, baby, and I'll be gone,
So long, so long, baby, so long.

So long, baby, so long, has my crow jane
  been gone?
How long, how long, baby, so long.

How long, baby, how long has my crow jane
  been . . .
So long, so long, baby, so long.

I was waitin' for that mail,
Hey-hey-hey, hey-hey-hey,
How long, so long, so long.

How long, how long am I to call you
  girl-of-my-own?
How long, how long, how long?

How long . . . am I to be treated wrong?
So long, so long, so long.

How long, baby, how long am I to be
  treated wrong?
How long, how long, baby, how long?

*Despite the title, James neither called nor considered this version
of a popular blues standard a "buck" (buckdance), but viewed the
titling as a mistake on the part of the company that recorded it.
†*jack*: a mule

Pay Day

Mississippi John Hurt

Yeah, I did all I can do, and I can't get along with you,
I'm gonna take you to your mama, Pay Day.

Chorus:
Pay Day, Pay Day . . .

Well, the rabbit in a log, I ain't got no rabbit dog,
And I hate to see that rabbit get away.

Chorus:
Get away . . .

Baby, did all I can do, and I can't get along with you,
I'm gonna take you to your mama, Pay Day.

Just about a week ago,
I'm gonna keep my skillet greasy if I can.

Chorus:
If I can, if I can . . .

(*Spoken:* You know what happened to me)
Well, the hounds is on my track, and the knapsack on my back,
I'm gonna make it to my shanty 'fore day.

Chorus:
'Fore day, 'fore day . . .

Baby, I did all I could do, an' I . . .
I'm gonna take you to your mama, Pay Day.

Well . . . and I ain't got no rabbit dog,
Lord, I hate to see that rabbit get away.

Chorus:
Get away . . .

Baby, I did all I can do, and I can't get along with you,
I'm gon' . . .

Pony Blues

Charlie Patton

Medium fast

Hitch ___ up my po - ny, sad - dle up my black mare.

Hitch ___ up my po - ny, sad - dle up my black mare.

I'm gon-na find a rid - er, ba - by, in the world some - where.

Hitch* up my pony, saddle up my black mare,
Hitch up my pony, saddle up my black mare,
I'm gonna find a rider, baby, in the world
   somewhere.

"Hello Central, the matter with your line?
Hello Central, matter, Lord, with your line?"
"Come a storm last night an' tore the
   wire down."

Got a brand new Shetland, man, already trained,
A brand new Shetland, baby, already trained,
Better get a little saddle, tie the loops†
   on your rein.

Ain't a brownskin woman like somethin'
   fit to eat?
Brownskin woman like somethin' fit to eat?
But a jet-black woman, don't put your hands
   on me.

Took my baby, go meet the mornin' train,
I took my baby, meet that mornin' train,
An' the blues come down, baby, like
   showers of rain.

I've got somethin' to tell you when I get
   the chance,
Somethin' to tell you when I get a chance,
I don't wanna marry, just wanna be your man.

*For reasons known only to himself, Patton pronounced "hitch" as
 though it were spelled "hit-itch."
†It is unclear whether Patton sings "tie the loops" or "tighten up."

120

Hammer Blues*

Charlie Patton

Medium slow

Gon-na buy me a ham-mock, car-ry it un-der-neath through the tree.

Gon-na buy my-self a ham-mock, gon-na car-ry it un-der-neath the tree._

So __ when the wind blow, the leaves_ may fall on me. ___

Gonna buy me a hammock, carry it underneath through the tree,
Gonna buy myself a hammock, gonna carry it underneath the tree,
So when the wind blow, the leaves may fall on me.

Go on, baby, you can have your way,
Ball on, baby, you can have your way,
Sister, every dog sure must have his day.

Got me shackled, I'm wearin' a ball and . . .
They've got me shackled, I'm wearin' my ball and chain,
An' they got me ready for that Parchman† train.

I went to the depot, I looked up at the board,
I went to the depot, I looked up at the board,
If this train has left, well, it's tearin' off up the road.

Clothes I buy, baby, honey, you gonna 'pre—, . . .
You're gonna appreciate, honey, all (the) clothes I'll buy,
I will give you all my lovin', baby, till the day I die.

I went way up Red River, crawlin' on the . . .
I went up Red River, crawlin' on a log,
I think I heard the *Bob Lee*‡ boat when she moaned.

*As the first verse indicates, this song was mistitled when it was
issued by Paramount Records.
†*Parchman:* the state prison in Parchman, Mississippi, whose
escapees often wandered into Patton's native Dockery, a Delta
plantation town.
‡*Bob Lee:* one of the steamships operated by the Lee Line of Memphis.

High Sheriff Blues

Charlie Patton

Medium fast

Get in trou-ble in Bel - zo - na, it ain't no use scream-in' and cry - in'. Hum - hum ___ Get in trou-ble · in Bel - zo - na, it ain't no use to scream-in' and cry - in'! Hum - hum ___ Mis - ter Webb will take you back to Bel - zo - na jail-house fly - in'.

Get in trouble in Belzona,* it ain't no use screamin' and cryin',
Get in trouble in Belzona, it ain't no use to screamin' and cryin',
Mr. Webb will take you back to Belzona jailhouse flyin'.

Let me tell you folkses how he treated me,
Let me tell you folkses how he treated me,
An' he put me in a cell, Lord, it was dark as it could be.

Lay there late one evenin', Mr. Purvis was standin' 'round,
Lay there late one evenin', Mr. Purvis was standin' 'round,
Mr. Purvis told Mr. Webb to let poor Charlie down.

It takes boozy boo', Lord, to cure these blues,
Takes boozy booze, Lord, to cure these blues,
But each day seems like years in a jailhouse where there is no boo'.

I got up one mornin', feelin' awful . . .
I got up one mornin', feelin' mighty bad,
Fella, it must not a-been them Belzona jail I had.
(*Spoken:* Blues I had, boys.)

Oh, Lord, in trouble, ain't no use to screamin' . . .
When I was in prison it 'tain't no use to screamin' and cry,
Mr. Purvis the onliest manager, he just pay no mind.

*The town of Belzoni, Mississippi, was originally named Belzona and was
so called until around 1920.

122

Woman Woman Blues

Moderately slow

Ishman Bracey

Wom-an, wom-an, wom-an, wom-an, Lord, what in the world you try-in' to do?___ Ba-by, the way___ ___ you treat me, break my heart in two.___

Woman, woman, woman, woman,
Lord, what in the world you tryin' to do?
Baby, the way you treat me, break my heart
    in two.

I've got a woman, pretty little woman,
She got coal-black, wavy hair,
Now, and everytime she smile, Lord, shines
    everywhere.

An' I've got a woman, pretty little woman,
She ain't anything but a stavin' chain,*
'Fraid she's a married woman and I'm scared
    to call her name.

Treat me like treat your baby,
Won't you shake me around and 'round?
Baby, when you lower me down, Lord, shake me
    down and 'round.

Now, these blue blues ain't nothin',
Lord, but a doggone, hungry spell,
Got no money in your pocket and you're
    surely catchin' hell.

Then I went, went to the depot,
Lord, I read up on the board,
Said, "If your baby ain't here, she'll be
    long ways up the road."

Now, I've got to studyin',† sittin' down studyin'
'Bout my old time used-to-be,
Lord, I've studied so hard, Lord, till these
    blues crept up on me.

*Stavin' Chain was the hero of several black toasts and folk tales,
legendary for his sexual prowess. His name either derived from
what was already a double entendre in black speech, or became
one as the result of the Stavin' Chain legend. "To stave" is to hammer, and the term "stavin' chain" is one of several country blues
idioms implying a relationship between sex and labor. In some
blues songs stavin' chain was a euphemism for penis; Bracey's
application of the term to the female sex is unique in blues. However, similar terms, such as "jelly roll," were applied to either sex,
or could describe sex itself.
†To study, in Southern speech, simply meant to ponder something.

You know what they say in *my* part of town, they tell you: a man's supposed to work for a woman; a woman ain't supposed to work for no man. Woman's supposed to just sit down, and a man do the work. I just say to myself, I say: "Goodnight, *Irene*! If you livin' with *me* you'll be workin'—if you don't you'll be on the soup line."

——Booker White

Outside Woman Blues

Blind Joe Reynolds

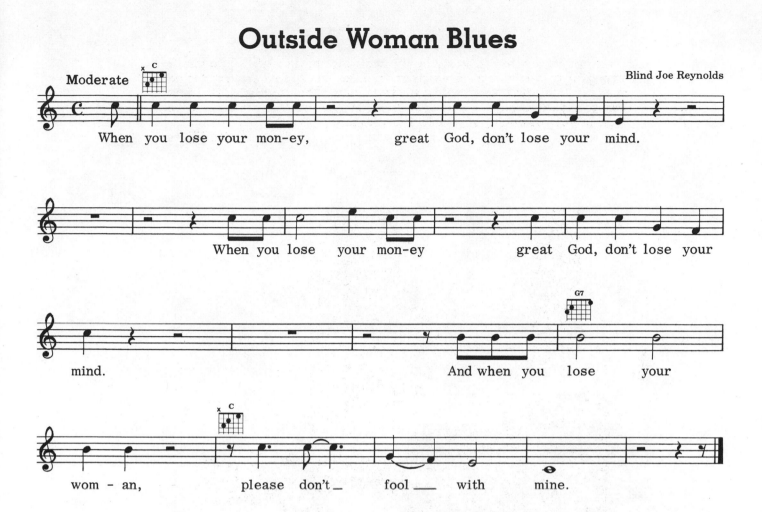

When you lose your money, great God, don't lose your mind,
When you lose your money, great God, don't lose your mind,
And when you lose your woman, please don't fool with mine.

I'm gonna buy me a bulldog, watch my old lady whilst I sleep,
I'm gonna buy me a bulldog, watch my old lady while I'm asleep,
'Cause women these days is so doggone crooked,
    till they might make a 'fore day creep.

Tell you married men how to keep young wives at home,
Tell you married men how to keep young wives at home,
Get you a job and roll for the man,* and try to carry your labor home.

Tell you married women how to keep your husbands at home,
Tell you married women how to keep your husbands at home,
You oughta take care of the man's labor and let these single boys alone.

You can't watch your wife and your outside women, too,
You can't watch your wife and your outside women, too,
While you're off with your woman, your wife could be at home
Beatin' you doin' it, buddy, what you tryin' to do?
Mmm, buddy, what you tryin' to do?

*the man: boss. If Reynolds is suggesting that in order to prevent infidelity
husbands must labor as hard in the bedroom as on the job, he is making the same
association between sex and toil remarked upon elsewhere in this volume.
Another ambiguous but intriguing blues use of the idea of "carrying" work
occurs in Frank Stokes's "Memphis Rounders Blues."

Police Dog Blues

Medium fast

Blind Blake

All ___ my life ___ I've been a trav - 'lin' man. ___

All ___ my life ___ I've been a trav - 'lin' man. ___

Stay - in' a - lone and do - in' the best I can. ___

All my life I've been a travelin' man,
All my life I've been a travelin' man,
Stayin' alone and doin' the best I can.

I shipped my trunk down to Tennessee,
I shipped my trunk down to Tennessee,
Hard to tell about a man like me.

I met a gal, I couldn't get her off my mind,
I met a gal, I couldn't get her off my mind,
She passed me up, said she didn't like my kind.

I'm scared to bother around her house
at night,
I'm scared to bother around her house
at night,
She got a police dog cravin' for a fight.

His name is "Rambler"—when he gets a chance,
His name is "Ramblin'"—when he gets a chance
He leave his mark on everybody's pants.

Guess I'll travel, I guess I'll let her be,
I guess I'll travel an' I guess I'll let her be,
Before she sics her police dog on me.

When You Got A Good Friend

Robert Johnson

Moderate

When you got a good friend that will stay right by your side.

When you got a good friend that will stay right by your side.

Give her all your spare time, try to love an' treat her right.

When you got a good friend that will stay right by your side,
When you got a good friend that will stay right by your side,
Give her all your spare time, try to love an' treat her right.

I mistreated my baby, I can't see no reason why,
I mistreated my baby, I can't see no reason why,
Every time I thinks about it I just wring my hands and cry.

Would the good old baby apologize or would she sympathize with me?
. . . or would she sympathize with me?
She's a brownskin woman, just as sweet as a girl friend can be.

I love my baby but I can't make that agee, (*sic*)
I love my woman but why can't we can't agree?
I really love that woman, wonder why we can't agree.

It's your opinion, friend-girl, that I may be right or wrong,
It's your opinion, friend-girl, that I may be right or wrong,
But when you watch your close friend, baby, then your enemies
  can't do you no harm.

When you got a good friend that will stay right by your side,
When you got a good friend that will stay right by your side,
Give her all of your spare time, try to love an' treat her right.

Weepin' Willow

Blind Boy Fuller
© Copyright 1944, J. Baxter Long
All Rights Reserved   Used by Permission

Lord, that weepin' willow and that mournin' dove,
That weepin' willow and that mournin' dove,
I got a gal up the country, Lord, you know I sure do love.

Now, if you see my woman, tell her I says hurry home,
(*Spoken:* Aw, sho')
You see my woman, tell her I says hurry home,
I ain't had no lovin' since my gal been gone.

Where it 'tain't no love, ain't no gettin' along,
Where it ain't no love, mama, ain't no gettin' along,
My gal treat me so mean and dirty, sometime I don't know right from wrong.

Lord, I lied down last night, tried to take my rest,
I lied down last night, tried to take my rest,
(*Spoken:* What happened, boy?)
You know, my mind got to ramblin' just like wild geese in the west.

Gonna buy me a bulldog, watch you whilst I sleep,
Gonna buy me a bulldog, watch you whilst I sleep,
Just to keep these men from makin' this early mornin' creep.

Now, if you see my woman, tell her I says hurry home,
You see my woman, tell her I says hurry home,
I ain't had no lovin' since my little gal been gone.

You gonna want my love, baby, some lonesome day,
(*Spoken:* Yeah!)
You gonna want my love, mama, some old lonesome day,
Then it be too late, I'll be gone too far away.

Walkin' Blues

Moderate

Robert Johnson

I woke up this morn-in', feel a-round for my shoes. Know by that I got these old walk-in' blues. I woke up this morn-in', feel-in' a-round for my shoes. But you know by that I've got these _ old walk-in' blues.

I woke up this mornin', feel around for my shoes,
Know by that I got these old walkin' blues.
I woke up this mornin', feelin' around for my shoe,
But you know by that I've got these old walkin' blue.

Lord, I feel my blowin' my old lonesome home,
Got up this mornin', now, little Bernice was gone.
Lord, I feel like blowin' my lonesome home,
Well, I got up this mornin', all I had was gone.

Well, leave this mornin' if I have to go ride the blind,
I've been mistreated an' I don't mind dyin'.
This morn' I have to ride the blind,
Babe, I been mistreated, baby, an' I don't mind dyin'.

Well! Some people tell me that the worried blues ain't bad,
Worst old feelin' I most ever had.
Some people tell me that these old worried old blues ain't bad,
It's the worst old feelin' I most ever had.

She got Elgin movements from her head down to her toes,
Break [Brake?] in on a dollar most anywhere she go.
. . . her head down to her toe,
(*Spoken:* Oh, honey!)
Lord, she break [brake?] in on a dollar most anywhere she go.

Richlands Women Blues*

Mississippi John Hurt
Copyright © 1963 Wynwood Music Co. Inc.
All Rights Reserved   Used by Permission

Moderate

Gim - me red lip - stick and a bright pur - ple rouge. A shin-gle-bob hair - cut and a shot of good boo'. Hur - ry down sweet dad - dy, come blow-in' your horn, If you come too late, sweet ma - ma will be gone. Come a - long young

Gimme red lipstick and a bright purple rouge,
A shingle-bob† haircut and a shot of good boo'.‡
Hurry down, sweet daddy, come blowin' your horn,
If you come too late, sweet mama will be gone.

Come along, young man, everythin's settin' right,
My husband's goin' away till next Saturday night.
Hurry down, sweet daddy, come blowin' your horn,
If you come too late, sweet mama will be gone.
Now, I'm rarin' to go, got red shoes on my feet,
My mind is sittin' right for a Tin Lizzie seat.
Hurry down, sweet daddy, come blowin' your horn,
If you come too late, sweet mama will be gone.

The red rooster said, "Cockle-doodle-do-do,"
The Richlands woman said, "Any dude will do."
Hurry down, sweet daddy, come blowin' your horn,
If you come too late, sweet mama will be gone.

With rosy red garters, pink hose on my feet,
Turkey red bloomer, with a rumble seat.
Hurry down, sweet daddy, come blowin' your horn,
If you come too late, sweet mama will be gone.

Every Sunday mornin', church (people?) watch me go,
My wings (are?) sprouted out, the preacher told me so.
Hurry down, sweet daddy, come blowin' your horn,
If you come too late, sweet mama will be gone.

Dress skirt cut high, then they cut low,
Don't think I'm a sport,** keep on watchin' me go.
Hurry down, sweet daddy, come blowin' your horn,
If you come too late, sweet mama will be gone.

Gimme red lipstick and a bright purple rouge,
A shingle-bob haircut and a shot of good boo'.
Hurry down, sweet daddy, come blowin' your horn,
If you come too late, sweet mama will be gone.

*Blues collector Dick Spottswood informs us that Hurt originally
performed this song at the request of William Meyers, a West
Virginian who planned to record it on his own privately produced
label around 1929. Since Meyers was a songwriter and the work
was a far cry from blues, it may have been Meyers' composition.
The Richlands in question is probably a small town (population
1300 in 1930) of the same name in southeastern Virginia.
†*shingle-bob:* a fashionable flapper's hair style of the twenties,
better known as "the shingle," and so named because the back
was clipped in layers.
‡*boo':* booze
**sport:* a passé term for a playboy or a party girl.

Pistol Blues

Crow Jane, Crow Jane, what makes you hold your head so high?— Ought-a just re-mem-ber, you got to live so long and die.———

Crow jane, crow jane, what makes you hold your head so high?
Oughta just remember, you got to live so long and die.

I'm gonna carry that woman through the weepin' willow tree,
For to hear her cryin', "Honey, don't murder me!"

I'm gonna slap her face, gonna drink that woman's rye,
Gonna kill that whiskey, pour the pistol dry.

She said, "Roll on,* jack, daddy do roll on!
Roll on, jack, daddy do roll on!"
She said, "Roll on, jack, daddy do roll on!
Like the way you rollin' but you ain't gonna roll for so long."

It ain't but two women (in the) world can swing my chain,
There ain't but two women, world, can swing my chain,
Ain't but two women, mama, can swing my chain,
That looks like Stella and that brown my jane.

Lord, Lord, look what my brown said to me,
Lord, Lord, look what she said to me,
Said Lord, Lord, look what she said to me,
Said, "When I leave this town I'm gonna carry you back with me."

*Here the meaning of "roll" is somewhat ambiguous, as it is on Blind Joe
Reynolds' "Outside Woman Blues" elsewhere in this collection. In everyday
Southern usage, "to roll" meant to work, as in the phrase "rolling cotton."
Like other expressions from the vocabulary of labor.("hauling ashes"), it
took on a sexual connotation in blues songs.

.20-20 Blues*

(Recorded under the title of ".22-20 Blues")*

Skip James
Copyright © 1965 Wynwood Music Co. Inc.
All Rights Reserved   Used by Permission

Last Verse: Hey, hey, hey,— hey, an' I can't take my rest.—

Hey, hey, hey, hey, I can't take my rest.— And my

for-ty-four— lay-in' up and down my breast.—

If I send for my baby and she don't come,
If I send for my baby and she don't come,
All the doctors in Wisconsin,† they won't help her none.

And if she gets unruly and gets so she don't wanna do,
My baby gets unruly and she don't wanna do,
I'll take my .32-20, I'll cut her half in two.

You're talkin' about your .44-40, buddy, it'll do very well,
Talkin' about your .44-40, it'll do very well,
But my .22-20, Lord, it's a burnin' hell.

I had a .38 Special, buddy, it's most too light,
Aw, that .38 Special, buddy, it's most too light,
But my .22-20 make the caps‡ all right.

Aw, if she gets unruly, thinks she don't wanna do,
She gets unruly and she don't wanna . . .
I'll take my .22-20, I'll cut her half in two.

Hey, hey, hey, hey, an' I can't take my rest,
Hey, hey, hey, hey, I can't take my rest,
And my .44 layin' up and down my breast.

*The ".22-20," which James saw as a simple rifle, doesn't properly exist. He opted for this caliber in meeting the studio request of a Paramount Records official for a "gun blues" that could be used to "cover" Roosevelt Sykes' successful ".44 Blues" on Okeh. If his rifle aim was no more accurate than his spontaneous versifying, which inadvertently evokes different caliber revolvers, it is safe to say that the unruly girlfriend of the song easily survived his barrage.
†This piece was originally recorded at Paramount's Grafton, Wisconsin studio.
‡caps: percussion caps

Try Me One More Time

Marshall Owens

Woke up this mornin', says, about two,
Had no other woman but I can't use you.
Cryin', "Try me one more time."
Cryin', "Try me one more time."
She said, "Take me back, try me one more time."

Woke up this mornin', said, about three,
The brown that I want got the chinch on me.
She's cryin', "Try me one more time."
She's cryin', "Try me one more time."
She said, "Take me back, try me one more time."

Woke this mornin', say, about four,
High brown knockin' on my back door.
She was cryin', "Try me one more time."
Cryin', "Try me one more time."
She said, "Take me back, try me one more time."

Woke this mornin', say, about five,
Can't get your woman, she tells too many lies.
She was cryin', "Try me one more time."
Cryin', "Try me one more time."
She said, "Take me back, try me one more time."

Woke this mornin' about the break of day,
Huggin' that pillow where my fair brown lay.
She's cryin', "Try me one more time."
Cryin', "Try me one more time."
She said, "Take me back, try me one more time."
Cryin', "Try me one more time."
Cryin', "Try me one more time."
She said, "Take me back, try me one more time."

Mama told me, daddy told me too,
"'Body grin in your face ain't no friend to you."
But she's cryin', "Try me one more time."
Cryin', "Try me one more time.
Take me back, try me one more time."

Travelin' Riverside Blues

Robert Johnson

Medium fast

If your man get per-son-al won't you have your fun?___ If your

man get per-son-al won't you have your fun?___ Says come (on) back

___ to Friar's Point ma - ma, an' bar-rel-house all night long. ___

If your man get personal, won't you have your fun?
If your man get personal, won't you have your fun?
Says, come on back to Friar's Point,* mama,
    an' barrelhouse all night long.

I've got womens in Vicksburg, clean on into Tennessee,
I've got womens in Vicksburg, clean on into Tennessee,
But my Friar's Point rider, now, hops all over me.

I ain't goin' to state no color but her front teeth crowned with gold,
I ain't goin' state no color but her front teeth is crowned with gold,
She got a mortgage on my body an' a lien on my soul.

Lord, I'm goin' to Rosedale,† gonna take my rider by my side,
Lord, I'm goin' to Rosedale, gonna take my rider by my side,
We can still barrelhouse, baby, 'cause it's on the riverside.

Now you can squeeze my lemon till the juice runs down my . . .
(*Spoken:* Till the juice runs down my leg,
    baby, you know what I'm talkin' about)
You can squeeze my lemon till juice runs down my bed,
(*Spoken:* That's what I'm talkin' about, now)
But I'm goin' back to Friar's Point if I be rockin' to my head.

*Friar's Point (population 998, 1930) is a riverside town in the Mississippi Delta.
†Rosedale (population 2000, 1930) is located forty miles south of Friar's Point.

Terraplane Blues*

Robert Johnson

Honey, I feel so lonesome, you hear me when I moan,
Honey, I feel so lonesome, you hear me when I moan,
Who been drivin' my Terraplane for you since I been gone?

I said, I flashed your lights, mama, your horn won't even blow,
(*Spoken:* Somebody done gone and messed with my machine!)
I even flashed my lights, mama, this horn won't even blow,
Had a short in this connection, whooh-well, it's way down below.

I'm gonna hoist your hood, mama, I'm bound to check your oil,
I'm gonna hoist your hood, mama, I'm bound to check your oil,
I've got a woman that I'm lovin' way down in Arkansas.

Now, you know the carbs ain't even buzzin',
Little generator won't even get the spark,
Oil's in a bad condition, you got to have these batteries charged.
I'm cryin', please, please don't do me wrong,
Who been drivin' my Terraplane now for you since I been gone?

Mister highway man, please don't block the road,
Please, please don't block the road,
'Cause she ridden a cold one hundred and I'm booked and I got to go.

*The Terraplane was one of the dominant cars in the low-priced market (it listed for
$595 in 1937), and its popularity has been credited with keeping Hudson Motors
afloat during the Depression.

(First line hummed)
. . . you hear me weep and moan,
Who been drivin' my Terraplane now for you since I been gone?

I'm gonna get deep down in this connection, keep on tanglin' with your wires,
I'm gonna get deep down in this connection, whooh-well, keep on tanglin' with these wires,
And when I mash down on your little starter, then your spark plugs will give me fire.

Number Three Blues

Buddy Boy Hawkins

I done lost all my money, (I) ain't got nowhere to go,
(I say) I done lost all my money, ain't got me nowhere to go,
I believe to my soul I'm 'bout to lose my brown.

All the women gets mad 'cause I won't "twa-twa-twa-twa,"
All you women gets mad 'cause I won't "twa-twa-twa-twa,"
All you women gets mad at Buddy Boy 'cause I won't "de-da-da-da."

I say, I flagged Number Four, mama, she kept on easin' me by,
I flagged Number Four, she kept on easin' me by,
I couldn't do anything, partner, but fold my little arms and cry.

Here come Number Three, with her headlights on top,
I say, here come Number Three, with her headlights on top,
I believe to my soul she's Alabama bound.

Apples on my table, peaches on my shelf,
Apples on my table, peaches on my shelf,
I've got to stay there to eat 'em all by myself.

Tom Rushen Blues*

Moderate   Charlie Patton

Laid down last night,_ hop-in' I would_ have my peace. (E - e)_

_ I laid down last night,_ hop-in' I would have my peace._ (E - e)_

_ But when I woke up, Tom Rush-en was_ shak-in' me.__

Laid down last night hopin' I would have my peace,
I laid down last night hopin' I would have my peace,
But when I woke up Tom Rushen was shakin' me.

When you get in trouble, it's no use to screamin' and cryin',
When you gets in trouble, it's no use go screamin' and cryin',
Tom Rushen will take you back to the prisonhouse flyin'.

It were late one night, Halloway was gone to bed,
It were late one night, Halloway was gone to bed,
Mister Day† brought whiskey taken from under Halloway's head.

An' it's boozy booze, now, Lord, to cure these blues,
It takes boozy boo', Lord, to cure these blues,
But each day seems like years in the jailhouse where there is no boo'.

I got up this mornin', Tom Day was standin' around,
I got up this mornin', Tom Day was standin' around,
If he lose his office now, he's runnin' from town to town.

Let me tell you folksies just how he treated me,
I'm gonna tell you folkses just how he treated me,
Aw, he caught me yellin', I was drunk as I could be.

*Tom Rushen was the town sheriff of Merigold, Mississippi, around the
 time Patton recorded this song.
†Tom Day had been Rushen's predecessor in office. This couplet
 undoubtedly remarks on the procedure of taking seized liquor to the
 county courthouse in order to establish proof of an illegal still.
 (Mississippi was a dry state until relatively recent days.)

Take Me Back Baby

Mance Lipscomb
Copyright © 1970 Tradition Music Co.
All Rights Reserved   Used by Permission

Oh ____ ba - by, take me back.

I won't do noth - in' you don't like. ____

2. Oh, I went down ____ that rail - road track ____

beg-gin' my ba - by ____ to ____ take me back.

Spoken:
Here's about the oldest number that I could recall, back in the days I was learnin' and heard people play, "Take Me Back."

Oh baby, take me back,
I won't do nothin' you don't like.

Oh, I went down that railroad track,
Beggin' my baby to take me back.

Take me back, me, one more time,
Won't do nothin' to worry your mind.

Tote your water and cut your wood,
Make your fire, if I could.

Oh baby, didn't you say
You're gonna lemme have my way?

'Tain't but the one thing grieve my mind,
My woman quit me in the wintertime.

Kill your chicken, baby, save me the wing,
Think I'm workin', ain't doin' a thing.

I got a girl, her name is Mar',
Works over yonder in the white folks' yard.

She rushed me chicken, rushed me a goose,
Precious little turkey, well it 'tain't no use.*

Take me back, take me back,
Won't do nothin', baby, you don't like.

*I.e., his tastes lean more toward turkey than to chicken or goose.

Stones In My Passway

. . . If you don't wanna go, don't prohibit me. Don't deprive me of *my* privilege. An' take my life. If you don't wanna be nothin' an' ain't got no foundation to build on, don't try to tear mine down. Let *me* build somethin' and let me go an' then perhaps I can reach back and get you if I get a few steps beyond you. But don't hinder me.

. . . There's a lots of people . . . don't wanna see you do nothin'. And if they can't prohibit your progress, lotta times your life will be taken from you. I don't know whether it's grudgery or onery, or just an ignorance to it, or just what. But I noticed that. But don't put that stumbling block in my path 'cause I'll leap it and go on by.

——Skip James

I got stones in my passway an' my road seem dark as night,
I got stones in my passway an' my road seem dark as night,
I have pains in my heart, they have taken my appetite.

I have a bird to whistle an' I have a bird to sing,
Have a bird to whistle an' I have a bird to sing,
I've got a woman that I'm lovin', boy, but she don't mean a thing.

My enemies have betrayed me, have overtaken poor Bob at last,
My enemies have betrayed me, have overtaken poor Bob at last,
An' it's one thing surely, they have stones all in my path.

Now, are you tryin' to take my life an' all my lovin', too?
You laid the passway for me, now what are you tryin' to do?
I'm cryin', please, please let us be friends,
An' when you hear me howlin' in my passway, rider,
Please open your door an' let me in.

I got three lanes to truck on, boys, please don't block my road,
I got three lanes to truck on, boys, please don't block my road,
I've feelin' ashamed 'bout my rider, baby, I'm booked an' I got to go.

Revenue Man Blues

These scoundrels would get down on their knees and stomachs and crawl through the thickets to those big outfits; two and three at a time. Never under that. And they be's well-armed, too: they carries high-powered rifles. Sometimes a rifle and two pistols apiece . . . Whenever the revenue mens come 'round and approach you like that, it's always best to give up, to surrender. 'Cause if you don't start shootin' *them*, understand, they'll really kill you.

And then some of them mollydodgers would drink that whiskey. Sure! They wouldn't report it all; keep some of it for themselves . . . Sometimes those guys would get some of those 'stilleries themselves . . . some of those scoundrels sell those things to a colored person.

——Skip James

Charlie Patton

Aw, the revenue men is ridin', boy, you'd better look out,
(*Spoken:* High sheriff ain't purty)
Aw, the revenue men is ridin', boy, you'd better look out,
(*Spoken:* Boy, if he hollers you—you don't stop, boy)
If he hollers you—don't stop, you will likely be knocked out.

Oh, a donay love saltwater,* well, she always wants a drink,
(*Spoken:* Got to have a drink!)
A donay love saltwater, she always wants a drink,
(*Spoken:* Boy, if they see you with a bottle, though)
If they see you with a bottle, they will almost break your neck.

*A "donay" is defined by Son House as a "no-good woman";
"saltwater" is an archaic synonym for alcohol.

Go safe sweet home through, Lord, that shiny star,
(*Spoken:* Aw sho'!)
I say, safe sweet home through that shiny star,
(*Spoken:* She don't need no tellin's, daddy, aw sho')
She don't need no tellin', daddy will take you in his car.

Oh, come on, mama, let us go to the edge of town,
(*Spoken:* Aw sho'!)
Come on, mama, let us go to the edge of town,
(*Spoken:* Baby, I know where there's a bird nest built at)
I know where there's a bird's nest built down on the ground.

Oh, I wake up every mornin' now, with a jinx all around my bed,
(*Spoken:* Aw sho'!)
I wakes up every mornin' with a jinx all around my bed,
(*Spoken:* You know I'll have them jinx forever!)
I have been a good provider but I believe I have been misled.

Nashville Stonewall Blues

Robert Wilkins

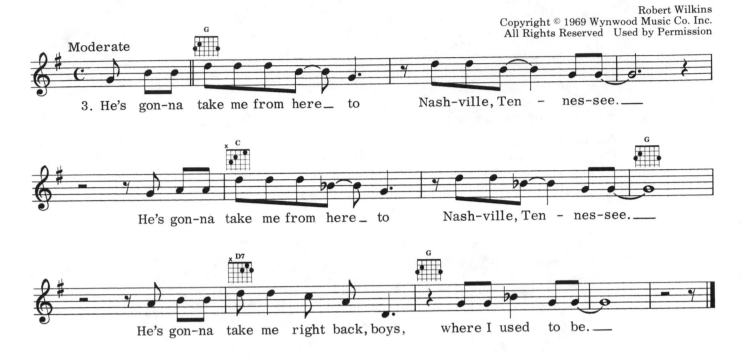

3. He's gon-na take me from here to Nash-ville, Ten - nes-see.

He's gon-na take me from here to Nash-ville, Ten - nes-see.

He's gon-na take me right back, boys, where I used to be.

I stayed in jail, it was for thirty long days, (twice)
And that woman said she loved me, I could not see her face.

I looked out the window, saw the long-chain man, (twice)
Aw, he's comin' to call the boys name by name.

He's gonna take me from here to Nashville, Tennessee, (twice)
He's gonna take me right back, boys, where I used to be.

I got a letter from home, reckon how it read?
I got a letter from home, reckonin' how it read?
It said, "Son, come on home to your mama, she's sick and nearly dead."

I sit down and cried, and I screamed and squalled, (twice)
Said, "I cannot come home, mama, I'm behind these walls."

Every mornin' 'bout four, boys, my deed have passed, (twice)
You oughta see me down in the foundries, tryin' to do my task.

'Cause the judge he sentenced me, boys, from five to ten, (twice)
I get out, I'm gonna kill that woman, I'll be right back again.

Charlie James

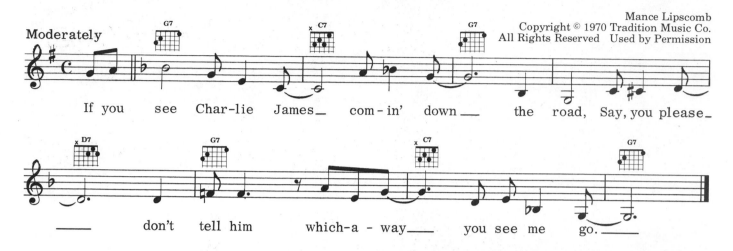

If you   see   Char-lie   James_ com-in'   down _ the   road, Say, you please_

_ don't   tell him   which-a - way_ you see me   go. _

If you see Charlie James comin' down the road,
Say you, please don't tell him which a-way you
     see me go.

In the mornin' soon, in the mornin' soon,
Yes, I'm goin' back to Houston in the
     mornin' soon.

Had a whole lotta money one day, one day,
Next day I didn't have a dime.

Look down the road just as far as I could see,
And I thought I spied my old-time used-to-be.

In a whole lot of trouble one day, one day,
Next day I didn't know what to do.

Look down the road just as far as I could see,
And I thought I spied my old-time used-to-be.

When a man gets in trouble, everybody throws
     him down,
A killing for his friends and they won't
     come around.

Nobody ever knows you when you're down
     and out,
Ask 'em for a favor, they don't know what's
     all about.

Well, you may go, you may try to stay,
But you'll be back some old rainy day.

Strange Place Blues

Booker White
Copyright © 1964 Wynwood Music Co. Inc.
All Rights Reserved   Used by Permission

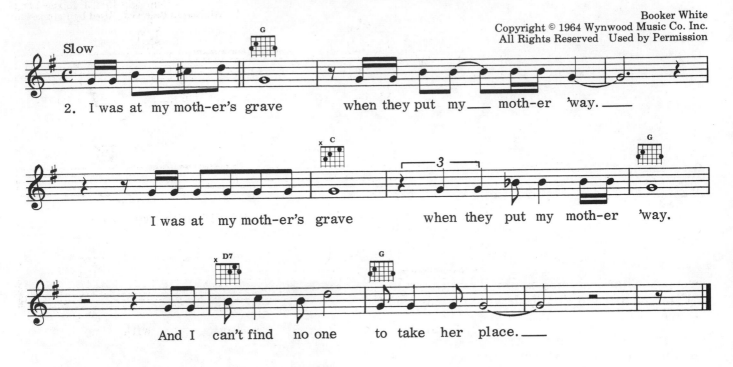

2. I was at my moth-er's grave when they put my__ moth-er 'way. __

I was at   my moth-er's grave   when they put my moth-er 'way.

And I   can't find   no one   to take   her   place.__

I'm a stranger at this place and I'm lookin' for my mother's grave,
I'm a stranger at this place and I'm lookin' for my mother's grave,
Well, it seems like to me, whoo-whoo well,* mama was throwed away.

I was at my mother's grave when they put my mother 'way,
I was at my mother's grave when they put my mother 'way,
And I can't find no one to take her place.

I thought after my mother was put away, I thought my wife would take her place,
After mama was put away I thought my wife would take her place,
. . . whoo-whoo well, my wife done throwed me away.

I wish I could find someone to take my mother's place,
I wish I could find someone to take my mother's place,
If I can't find no one, whoo-whoo well, you will find me at her grave.

I'm standin' on my mother's grave and I wished I could seen her face,
I'm standin' on my mother's grave and I wished I could seen her face,
I be glad when that day come,
    whoo-whoo well, when you women be through throwin' me away.

*The interjection "whoo-whoo well," partially sung falsetto, was popularized by Peetie
Wheatstraw. Robert Johnson also copies it on "Terraplane Blues" (*q.v.*).

Stingy Mama

Blind Boy Fuller
© Copyright 1944, J. Baxter Long
All Rights Reserved   Used by Permission

Medium slow

Stin - gy ma - ma, don't be so stin-gy with me.____ I say,

stin - gy ma - ma,____ don't be so stin-gy with me.____

Said you'se a good lit- tle girl,__ Lord you so stin - gy with me.

Stingy mama, don't be so stingy with me,
I say, stingy mama, don't be so stingy with me,
Said, you's a good little girl, Lord, you so stingy with me.

Throw your water out your pitcher, mama, let your bowl go dry,
Throw your water out your pitcher, let your bowl go dry,
Said, I want some of your lovin', mama, just before you die.

Said, my babe got a mojo* and she won't let me see,
Said, my babe got a mojo, she won't let me see,
One mornin' about four o'clock she eased that old thing on me.

Now mama, mama, you can't keep that mojo hid,
I say, hey-hey, mama, can't keep that mojo hid,
'Cause I got something, mama, just to find that mojo with.

Now my mama left me something called that old stingaree,†
Hey, mama left me somethin' called that stingaree,
Says, I done stung my little woman and she can't stay away from me.

*In its literal sense, a mojo was a conjurer's charm used to attract the affections of
  another person; its blues function as a sexual euphemism seems to have arisen
  with Blind Lemon Jefferson's "Low-Down Mojo" (1928).
†*stingaree*: stock blues euphemism for the sexual organs, usually applied to
  women and invariably appearing as a rhyme word.

Stagolee*

Mississippi John Hurt
Copyright © 1964 Wynwood Music Co. Inc.
All Rights Reserved   Used by Permission

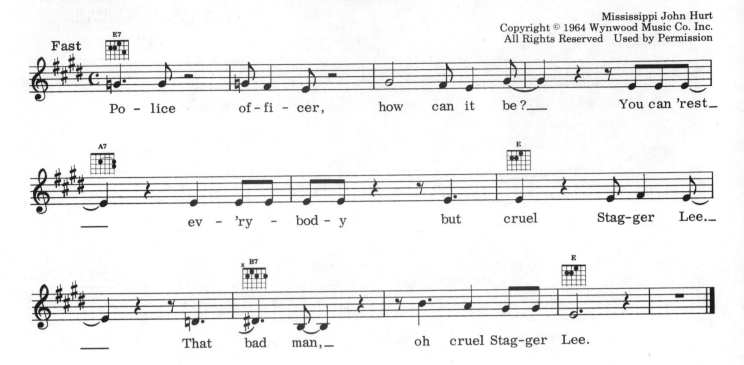

Po - lice of-fi - cer, how can it be?___ You can 'rest___ ___ ev - 'ry - bod - y but cruel Stag-ger Lee. ___ That bad man,— oh cruel Stag-ger Lee.

Police officer, how can it be?
You can 'rest everybody but cruel Stagger Lee.
That bad man, oh, cruel Stagger Lee.

Billy de Lyon told Stagger Lee, "Please don't take my life.
I got two little babies, and a darlin' lovin' wife."
That bad man, oh, cruel Stagger Lee.

"What I care about your two little babies, your darlin' lovin' wife?
You done stole my Stetson hat, I'm bound to take your life."
That bad man, cruel Stagger Lee.

Fourth and fifth verses hummed.

. . . with the forty-four.
When I spied Billy de Lyon, he was lyin' down on the floor.
That bad man, oh cruel Stagger Lee.

"Gentlemans of the jury, what you think of that?
Stagger Lee killed Billy de Lyon about a five-dollar Stetson hat."
That bad man, oh, cruel Stagger Lee.

And all they gathered, hands way up high,
At twelve o'clock they killed him, they's all glad to see him die.
That bad man, oh, cruel Stagger Lee.

*Despite his popularity as the anti-hero of this traditional song and of a Negro toast, "Stagger Lee" (or "Stack O'Lee," as he was sometimes called) has no known historical identity. The name may derive from the *Stacker Lee*, the third of fourteen steamships built by the Lee Line of Memphis, all of which were named after children of the owner. It ran between Memphis and Friar's Point, Mississippi, and first saw service sometime before 1890. Robert Wilkins' "Alabama Blues" (*q.v.*) contains a reference to the same ship.

Shake Shake Mama

(Cherry Ball)

Mance Lipscomb
Copyright © 1970 Tradition Music Co.
All Rights Reserved   Used by Permission

Oh, ain't gon - na give __ you no more cher-ry ball. __

Oh, ain't gon - na give you no more cher - ry ball. __

You gone drunk and showed your San - ta Claus. __

Oh, ain't gonna give you no more cherry ball,
Oh, ain't gonna give you no more cherry ball,
You gone drunk and showed your Santa Claus.*

Oh, a little bitty woman, hips just like a snake,†
Oh, a little bitty woman, her hip just like
  a snake,
. . . baby, it really take.

Oh, late last night my love come fallin' down,
Me and my baby on our last go-'round.

Oh, shake, shake mama, I'll buy you
  a diamond ring,
Oh, shake, shake mama, I'll buy you
  a diamond ring,
You don't shake, ain't gonna buy you
  a doggone thing.

Oh, my clutch start to slippin', carbs won't
  even sing,
Oh, my clutch start to slippin', my carbs won't
  even sing,
Blues in the compression, fire my piston ring.

Oh, rider, you ain't foolin' me,
Lookey here, rider, you ain't foolin' me,
You been slippin' to your old-time used-to-be.

Oh, I like my babe but I don't like
  her teddy bear,‡
Oh, I like my woman but I don't like
  her teddy bear,
I'm gonna buy her a box-back, maybe it'll work.

*One of the country blues' least common sexual euphemisms,
 "Santa Claus" may have an idiomatic basis in Southern speech.
 Tossing a quarter to an elderly Negro, a Faulkner character remarks, "Buy yourself some Santy Claus."
†*hips just like a snake:* said of people who twirl their bodies
 impressively.
‡*teddy bear:* a woman's one-piece undergarment, worn in the
 twenties.

Moon Goin' Down

Medium fast

Charlie Patton

Aw that moon has gone down ba - by, — North Star 'bout to shine. —

Aw that moon go - in' down ba - by, North Star 'bout to shine. —

Ros - et - ta Hen - ry — told me: "Lord, I

don't want you hang - in' 'round. —

Aw, that moon has gone down, baby, North Star 'bout to shine,
Aw, the moon goin' down, baby, North Star 'bout to shine.
Rosetta Henry told me, "Lord, I don't want you hangin' 'round."

Oh well, where were you now, baby, Clarksdale mill burned down?*
Oh well, where were you now, babe, Clarksdale mill burned down?
(*Spoken:* Boy, you know where I were)
"I were way down Sunflower† with my face all fulla frowns."

They's a house over yonder, painted all over green,
They's a house over yonder, painted all over green.
(*Spoken:* Boy, you know I know it's over there!)
Some of the finest young women, Lord, a man most ever seen.

Lord, I think I heard the Helena whistle, Helena whistle,
    Helena whistle blow,
Lord, I think I heard the Helena whistle blow.
(*Spoken:* Well, I hear it blowin' now)
Lord, I ain't gonna stop walkin' till I get in my rider's door.

*The upper Mississippi Delta town of Clarksdale suffered a serious fire in 1899.
†Whether Patton means the river, the town, or the county of Sunflower is
    unclear.

Lord, the smokestack is black and the bell it shine like,
  bell it shine like, bell it shine like gold,
Aw, the smokestack is black and the bell it shine like gold.
(*Spoken:* Shuckin' boy, you know it looks good to me)
Lord, I ain't gonna walk here, tarry around no more.

Hey, hey, evenin' was at midnight when I heard the local blow,
Aw, was evenin' at midnight when I heard the local blow.
(*Spoken:* Boy, I'm gettin' lonesome . . .)
I got to see my rider when she gettin' on board.

Mississippi Moan

The Mississippi Moaner

Medium fast

2. When she come in rag tied on her head.

She ___ come in ___ rag tied on her head. _(Spoken:) Asked my_ ba-

- by two ques-tions, she swore she _ was near-ly dead. ___

Hey, somethin' goin' on wrong,
Know, when I come in, find my baby gone.

When she come in, rag tied on her head,
She come in, rag tied on her head,
(*Spoken:* Asked my) baby two questions, she
    swore she was nearly dead.

I said, treat me good, Lord bless your soul,
Treat me good, Lord bless your soul,
If you treat me bad, mama, to hell you'll
    surely go.

Said, I'm on my way back to that lonesome hill,
On my way back to that lonesome hill,
'Cause that's where I can look down where
    this black man* used to live.

Aw, shall become of me?
I said, mama, what's gonna become of me?
Every time I leave home, says, I'm gonna
    follow that bumblebee.†

Lord, my bumblebee, mama, caused me to leave
    my old home,
Bumblebee have caused me to leave my home,
Lord, I tried and I tried and I just can't
    let her alone.

this black man: the artist himself. A similar use of "this" in other
 phrases was once considered a peculiarity of Negro dialect.
†The idea of a lover as a bumblebee was popularized by Memphis
 Minnie's 1930 recording, "Bumble Bee."

See See Rider

Arranged by Mance Lipscomb
Copyright © 1972 Tradition Music Co.
All Rights Reserved   Used by Permission

See, see rid-er, _____ see what you done done. ____

See, see rid-er, see what you _ done done. _

See, see rid-er, see what you_ done done. __ You done made_

_ me love you, hon-ey, now your man done come. __ I'm goin'

See, see, rider, see what you done done, (three times)
You done made me love you, honey, now your man done come.

I'm goin' to Louisiana, you know that's across the line,*
Goin' to Louisiana, you know that's across the line,
Goin' to Louisiana, you know that's across the line,
I'll be seldom seen, baby, and hard to find.

If I had two women and my partner didn't have none,
If I had two women and my partner didn't have none,
Had two women an' my partner didn't have none,
I'd take one of my women and give my partner one.

Soon one mornin', blues knocked on my door,
Soon one mornin', the blues knocked on my door,
Oh, soon one mornin', the blues knocked on my door,
"Come here to stay with you, won't be leavin' no more."

*Lipscomb is a native of Texas.

See See Rider

Mississippi John Hurt
Copyright © 1963 Wynwood Music Co. Inc.
All Rights Reserved   Used by Permission

You see, see, rider, you see what you have done?
You made me love you . . .
Made me love you, now your man done come,
You made me love you, now your man have come.

Ain't no more potatoes, the frost have killed the vine,
Well, the blues ain't nothin' but a good woman on your mind,
The blues ain't nothin' but a good woman on your mind,
The blues ain't nothin' but a good woman on your mind.

You see, see, rider, you see what you done?
You done made me love you . . .
You made me love you . . .

I've told you, baby, and your mama told you, too,
"You're three times seven, you know what you wanna do,
Three times seven, you know what you wanna do,
You're three times seven, you know what you wanna do."

If I hadda listened to my second mind,
Lord, I wouldn'ta been sittin' here and wringin' my hands and cryin',
I wouldn't been sittin' here, wringin' my hands and cryin',
I wouldn't been sittin' here, wringin' my hands and cryin'.

You see, see, rider, you see what you have done?
You done made me love you . . .
You made me love you . . .

Screamin' And Hollerin' The Blues

Charlie Patton

Girl, my ma-ma's get-tin'___ old,___ her head is turn-in' grey.___ For my ma-ma's get-tin' old, head is___ turn-in'___ grey. Don't you know it'll break her heart,___ know, my liv-in' this a-way?

Jackson on a high hill, mama, Natchez just below,*
Jackson on a high hill, mama, Natchez just below,
I ever get back home, I won't be back no more.

Girl, my mama's gettin' old, (her) head is turnin' gray,
For my mama gettin' old, head is turnin' gray,
Don't you know it'll break her heart, know, my livin' this a-way?

Ever woke up in the mornin', jinx all around your bed?
Ever woke up in the mornin', jinx all around your bed?
(*Spoken:* Children, I know how it is, baby)
Turned my face to the wall an' I didn't have a word to say.

No use a-hollerin', no use screamin' and cryin',
No use of hollerin', no use of screamin' and cryin',
For you know you got a home, mama, long as I got mine.

Hey, Lord have mercy on my wicked soul,
Oh, Lord have mercy on my wicked soul,
I wouldn't mistreat you, baby, for my weight in gold.

Goin' away, baby, don't you wanna go?
I'm goin' away, sweet mama, don't you wanna go?
(*Spoken:* I know you wanna go, baby!)
Take God to tell when I be back here anymore.

*The unintelligible vocal aside that follows this line is probably a
disclaimer, since it is Vicksburg that blues singers conventionally
(and correctly) situate on the high hill.

Frankie*

Mississippi John Hurt
Copyright © 1964 Wynwood Music Co. Inc.
All Rights Reserved   Used by Permission

Frank-ie was a good girl,___ ev-'ry-bod-y know, She paid one hun-dred dol-lars___ for Al-bert's suit of clothes.___ ___ He's her man___ but he did her wrong.___

Spoken Introduction:

"Frankie and Albert," the same thing as "Frankie and Johnnie."

Frankie was a good girl, everybody know,
She paid one hundred dollars for Albert's suit of clothes.
He's her man, but he did her wrong.

Frankie went down to the corner saloon, she ordered her a glass of beer,
She asked the barkeeper, "Has my lovin' Albert been here?"
"He been here, but he's gone again."

"Ain't gonna tell you no story, Frankie, I ain't gonna tell you no lie."
Says, "Albert a-passed about a hour ago, with a girl you call Alice Frye.
He's your man, and he's doin' you wrong."

Frankie went down to the corner saloon, she didn't go to be gone long,
She peeked through keyhole in the door, spied Albert in Alice's arm.
"He's my man, and he's doin' me wrong."

Frankie called Albert, Albert says, "I don't hear."
"If you don't come to the woman you love, gonna haul you outta here.
He's my man, and you's doin' me wrong."

Frankie shot old Albert, she shot him three or four times.
Says, "Stand back, I'm smokin' my gun, let me see is Albert dyin'.
He's my man, and he did me wrong."

Frankie and the judge walked outta the stand, and walked out side by side.
The judge says, "Frankie, you're gonna be justified.
Killin' a man, and he did you wrong."

*Perhaps unintentionally, this song expresses a particle of cynical wisdom once
current among blues singers—that betrayal of a "hustlin' woman" who
fosters a love affair with material gifts is suicidal. The same point of view seems
to underlie Robert Johnson's "Kindhearted Woman Blues."

Frankie was a good girl, everybody know,
She paid one hundred dollars for Albert's suit of clothes.
He's her man, and he did her wrong.

Said, "Turn me over, mother, turn me over slow,
It may be my last time, you won't turn me no more.
He's my . . ."

Says, Frankie was a good girl, everybody know,
She paid one hundred dollars for Albert's suit of clothes.
He's her man, and he did her wrong.

Lost Lover Blues

Blind Boy Fuller
© Copyright 1944, J. Baxter Long
All Rights Reserved   Used by Permission

Says I went down, by that freight de - pot, and that freight it come roll - in' by.. Lord, and I sure ain't got no lov - in' ba - by now. And I sure ain't got no lov - in' ba - by now.

Says, I went down by that freight depot,
And that freight, it come rollin' by.
Lord, and I sure ain't got no lovin' baby now,
And I sure ain't got no lovin' baby now.

Then I went off in that far distant land,
I weren't there long 'fore I got a telegram.
(*Spoken:* What'd it say?)
Sayin', "Now man, won't you please come home?
Now man, won't you please come home?"

Then I went back home, I looked on the bed,
And that best ol' friend I had was dead.
Lord, and I ain't got no lovin' baby now.
And I ain't got no lovin' baby now.

Then I'm sorry, sorry, sorry to my heart,
But the best of friends someday must part.
Lord, I ain't got no lovin' baby now,
And I ain't got no lovin' baby now.
(*Spoken:* Play it for me, now.)

Now as sure as the bird friends
    in the sky above,
Life ain't worth livin' if you ain't with
    the one you love.
Lord, and I got no lovin' baby now,
Lord, I ain't got no lover now.

If I knowed she didn't love me and didn't
    want me, too,
I would take morphine and die.
Lord, I ain't got no lovin' baby now,
And I ain't got no lovin' baby now.

Poor Me

Charlie Patton

Yes on me, it's poor me, you must take pity on poor me,
I (ain't) got nobody, take pity on poor me.
You may go, you may stay, but she'll come back some sweet day,
By and by, sweet mama, by and by.

Don't the moon look pretty shinin' down through the tree?
Oh, I can see Bertha Lee,* Lord, but she can't see me.
You may go, you may stay, but she'll come back some sweet day,
By and by, sweet mama, baby won't you, by and by?

You may go, you may stay, but she'll come back some sweet day,
By and by, sweet mama, by and by.
Yes on me, poor me, you must have pity on poor me,
I ain't got me nobody, take pity on poor me.

Don't the moon look pretty shinin' down through the tree?
Oh, I can see Bertha Lee, but she can't see me.
You may go, you may stay, but she'll come back some sweet day,
By and by, sweet mama, oh baby, won't you, by and by?

*Bertha Lee was Patton's girl friend and recording partner in the early 1930's.

Pony Blues

Son House
© Copyright 1941 by Sondick Music Company
All Rights Reserved   Used by Permission

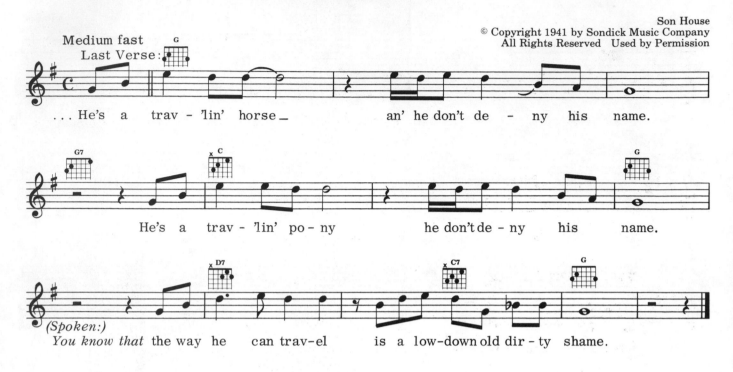

Medium fast
Last Verse:

...He's a trav-'lin' horse _ an' he don't de-ny his name.

He's a trav-'lin' po-ny he don't de-ny his name.

(Spoken:)
You know that the way he can trav-el is a low-down old dir-ty shame.

First verse hummed.

Why don't you catch* my pony, now saddle up my black mare?
. . . my pony, saddle up, up my black mare?
You know, I'm gonna find my baby, well, in the world somewhere.

You know, he's a travelin' horse, an' he's too black bad,†
He's a travelin' pony, I declare, he's too black bad.
You know, he got a gait, now, no Shetlan' ain't never had.

You know, I taken him by the rein an' I led him around and 'round,
I say, I taken him by the reins an' I—I led him, him 'round and 'round.
You know, he ain't the best in the world, but he's the best ever been in this town.

You know, he's a travelin' horse and he don't deny his name,
He's a travelin' pony and he don't deny his name.
You know, the way he can travel is a low-down, old, dirty shame.

Why don't you come up here, pony, now come on, please let's us go,
I said, "Come up, get up now, please pony, now let's us go."
Let's we saddle on down on the Gulf of, of Mexico.

You know, the horse that I'm ridin', he can fox-trot, he can lope and pace,
I say, the pony I'm ridin', he can fox-trot, he can lope and pace.
You know, a horse with them many gaits, you know, I'm bound to win the race.

. . . He's a travelin' horse an' he don't deny his name,
He's a travelin' pony, he don't deny his name.
(Spoken: You know that) the way he can travel is a low-down, old, dirty shame.

*catch: probably, to rig up to a buggy.
†too black bad: vague blues superlative, along the order of "mean" or "too tight."
  Although the tendency to invert conventional meaning has been described as a
  characteristic of black phrase-mongering, this expression has precedent in passé
  phrases like "bad to beat," meaning hard to beat. "Black" belongs in House's
  phrase as an intensifier, or else is used for the sake of alliteration.

Police Sergeant Blues

Robert Wilkins
Copyright © 1969 Wynwood Music Co. Inc.
All Rights Reserved   Used by Permission

I'm gonna tell you, baby, tell you now,
If you don't want me, you don't have to dog me around.
Because that old girl's mad with me, friend, but I don't care,
'Cause that old girl's mad with me, friends, but I don't care.

Now looka yonder, baby, what I see?
A police and a sergeant, they is comin' after me.
Because that old girl's mad with me, friends, but I don't care.

I'm gonna tell you that I'm forceted to take the ride,
When you see me goin', baby, hang your head and cry.
Because that old girl's mad with me, friends, but I don't care.

I'm gonna tell the judge that I know that I done wrong,
You go and get some lawyers to come and go my bond.
Because that old girl's mad with me, friends, but I don't care.

I know the judge is gonna give me thirty long days,
I made it up in my mind, baby, to go and stay.
Because that old girl's mad with me, friend, but I don't care.

I'm going out and work out my time,
Because the girl I love, she's not got a dime.
Because that old girl's mad with me, friends, but I don't care.

.32-20 Blues*

Robert Johnson

If I send for my baby, man, and she don't come,
If I send for my baby, man, and she don't come,
All the doctors in Hot Springs sure can't help her none.

An' if she gets unruly, thinks she don't wanna do,
If she gets unruly an' thinks she don't wanna do,
Take my .32-20, now, an' cut her half in two.

She got a .38 Special but I believe it's most too light,
She got a .38 Special but I believe it's most too light,
I got a .32-20 got to make the caps all right.

If I send for my baby, man, an' she don't come,
If I send for my baby, man, an' she don't come,
All the doctors in Hot Springs sure can't help her none.

I'm gonna shoot my pistol, gonna shoot my Gatling gun,
I'm gonna shoot my pistol, got to shoot my Gatling gun,
You made me love you, now your man have come.

Oh, baby, where you stay last night?
Oh, baby, where you stay last night?
You got the hair all tangled, an' you ain't talkin' right.

Her .38 Special, boys, it do very well,
Her .38 Special, boys, it do very well,
I got a .32-20 now, an' it's a burnin' . . .

If I send for my baby, man, an' she don't come,
If I send for my baby, man, an' she don't come,
All the doctors in Wisconsin sure can't help her none.

*A former owner of such a weapon describes it as a long-barreled
rifle, capable of firing a .44 slug.

Hey, hey, baby, where you stay last night?
Hey, hey, baby, where you stay last night?
You didn't come home until the sun was shinin' bright.

Aw, boys, I just can't take my rest,
Aw, boys, I just can't take my rest
With this .32-20 layin' up and down my breast.

Lazy Blues

Moderately slow

Mississippi John Hurt
Copyright © 1964 Wynwood Music Co. Inc.
All Rights Reserved   Used by Permission

Wake up in the morn-in' with a tow-el tied 'round her head.

Wake up ___ in the morn-in' tow-el tied 'round_ her head._

When you speak _ to her you swear she al-most dead._

Wake up in the mornin', with a towel tied 'round her head,
Wake up in the mornin', towel tied around her head,
When you speak to her you swear she almost dead.

Well, tell me, baby, what make you walk so slow?
Oh, tell me, baby, what make you walk so slow?
"Well, I feel just like I never felt before."

Pea Vine Blues*

Charlie Patton

I think I heard the Pea Vine when it blowed,
I think I heard the Pea Vine when it blowed,
It blow just like my rider gettin' on board.

Well, the levee sinkin', you know I, baby . . .
(*Spoken:* Baby, you know I *can't* stay!)
The levee is sinkin', Lord, you know I cannot . . .
I'm goin' up the country, mama, in a few more days.

Yes, you know it, she know it, she know you done done me wrong,
Yes, you know it, you know it, you know you done done me wrong,
Yes, you know it, you know it, you know you done done me wrong.

Yes, I cried last night and I ain't gonna cry anymore,
I cried last night an' I, I ain't gonna cry anymore,
'Cause the Good Book tells us you've got to reap just what you sow.

Stop your way o' livin' an' you won't . . .
(*Spoken:* You won't have to cry no more, baby!)
Stop your way o' livin' an' you won't have to cry anymore,
Stop your way 'o' livin' an' you won't have to cry anymore.

I think I heard the Pea Vine when it blowed,
I think I heard Pea Vine when it blowed,
She blowed just like she wasn't gonna blow no more.

*Pea Vine: A Mississippi Delta train on the famous "Dog" (Y&MV) line.

Parchman Farm Blues*

Booker White
Copyright © 1969 Wynwood Music Co. Inc.
All Rights Reserved   Used by Permission

Medium fast

Judge gim-me life this morn-in' down on Parch-man Farm.

Judge gim-me life this morn-in' down on Parch-man Farm._ I would-n't

hate it so bad but I tells my wife _ this morn. __

Judge gimme life this mornin' down on Parchman Farm,
Judge gimme life this mornin' down on Parchman Farm.
I wouldn't hate it so bad, but I tells my wife this morn':

"Oh, good-bye, wife, all you have's done gone,
Oh, good-bye, wife, all you have's done gone.
But I hope some day you will hear my lonesome song."

Oh, you listen, you men, I don't mean no harm,
Oh, oh, listen, you men, I don't mean no harm.
If you wanna do good, you better stay offa old Parchman Farm.

We go to work in the mornin', just the dawn of day,
We go to work in the mornin', just the dawn of day.
Just at the settin' of the sun, that's when the work is done.

I'm down on old Parchman Farm, and I sure wanna go back home,
I'm down on old Parchman Farm, but I sure wanna go back home.
But I hope someday I will overcome.

*Mississippi's Parchman Farm was founded and operated as a
profit-making plantation, the prisoners producing cotton crops for
the state. Despite this dubious function, inmates were permitted
conjugal visits as far back as the twenties; and the privileges
extended to trustees later became an item of government scandal.
The artist himself, who claims to have enjoyed trustee status while
an inmate during the mid-thirties, today looks back upon his
Parchman experience with acute nostalgia.

On My Last Go Round

Joe Callicott
Copyright © 1969 Uncle Doris Music, Ltd. (United Kingdom)
65 Parkway, London, N.W.1 7PP.—U.S.A. controlled by
Uncle Doris Music, Inc. 165 West 74th Street, New York 10023
All Rights Reserved   Used by Permission

Spoken:
Look out, here. . . . Don't shout over there, now. . . .
Leavin' town now.

I been crawlin', monkeyin' around all night long,
I been crawlin', monkeyin' around all night long.
It's done come my hour to show you right from wrong.

I walked to my window and, and back to my door,
(*Spoken:* Yeah!)
I walked to my window, I walked to my door.
Oh well, the Good Book teach me: got to reap just what I sow.

I'm tellin' you, good buddy, poor Joe, on his last go-'round,
I tell you, buddy, on my last go-'round,
Now I smell your bread burnin', baby, and turn your damper down.

Well, I rolled and I tumbled, and I cried all night long,
Well, I rolled, I tumbled, and I cried all night long.
I didn't have nobody to teach poor Joe right from wrong.

. . . moanin' low,
. . . Why ain't you moanin' low?
Now the Good Book teach you, woman: got to reap just what you sow.

Lonesome Atlanta Blues

Bobby Grant

I'm ____ so lone-some, got so lone-some, hear me cry-ing, ba-by, I ain't ly-ing. I'm so lone-some, got those lone-some At-lan-ta blues. I'm so ____ ____ sad and lone-some, ma-ma I don't know what to do. ____

I'm so lonesome, got so lonesome, hear me cryin', baby, I ain't lyin',
I'm so lonesome, got those lonesome Atlanta blue,
I'm so sad and lonesome, mama, I don't know what to do.

When you have a feelin', that mean old feelin',
    that dirty old feelin', ummm, that feelin',
When you have a feelin' that your gal don't want you no more,
You just might as well leave her, even if it hurts you so.

I'm gonna walk down the dirt road, that long, long dirt road,
    that dirty old dirt road, ummm, that dirt road.
I'm gonna walk down the dirt road, till somebody lets me ride,
If I can't find my baby, I'll run away and hide.

I'm goin' back to Atlanta, I mean down in Georgia,
    crazy about Atlanta, I mean Atlanta, Georgia.
I'm goin' back to Atlanta, down on Decatur Street,
If I can't find my baby, aw, be so kind to me.

Married Woman Blues

Joe Callicott

Well, I love my woman, don't care what she do,
Well, I love my baby, don't care what she do.
All I ask you, good girl, to be kind and true.

Well, I always tell when your woman gonna treat you mean,
You can always tell when your woman gon' treat you mean.
Get your meals unregular, house ain't never clean.

Goin' away to leave you, hang crepe on your door,
Well, I'm going away to leave you, hang crepe on your door.
Says, I won't be dead, comin' back no more.

Well, I hit my little girl, says, with a single-tree,
Aw, little girl, I hit my little woman with a single-tree.
Well, you mighta heard her hollerin', "Don't you murder me."

Spoken:
Play it one time, 'tween it.

Well, I hit that girl again, says, and I blackened her eye,
Well, I hit that woman again, says, and I blackened her eye.
? . . I's scared she'd die.

Well, I love that woman, says, I love her for myself, doggone yes,
I love that woman, I love her for myself.
Say, if she don't have me, don't have nobody else.

Well, I'm goin' to the racetrack, see my pony run,
Yes, baby, I'm going to the racetrack, see my pony run.
Say, if I wins any money, I'm gonna save you some.

Spoken:
Play it again.

Well the ? they're makin', now it done got most too strong,
Say the whiskey they makin', now it's gettin' too strong.
(*Spoken:* Look like to me I wanna go along)
Say, if you drink much of it, swear you can't go along.

I'm going, baby, ain't gonna be here no more,
I'm . . . I ain't gonna be here no more.
Say, if you didn't mistreat me, like you done before.

She's a married woman, says, I stole her from her man,
She's a married woman, I stole her from her man.
Says, I'm runnin' around, just from hand to hand.

Aw, sometime I think I got the sweetest girl in town,
(*Spoken:* Get right)
Aw, sometime I think I got the sweetest girl in town.
She's tailor-made and she ain't no hand-me-down.

Well, my time done come, says I'll, I believe I'll go,
Now my time done come, I believe I'll go.
Ain't gonna be one woman's dirty dog no more.

Oh, I'm going away to leave you, hang crepes all over your door,
Sweet baby . . .

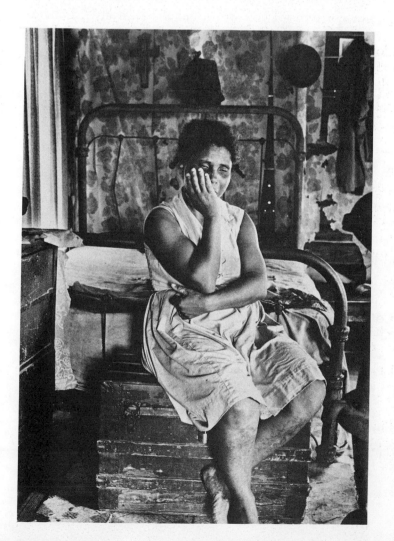

Mississippi Bo Weavil*

When I was a kid we had a depression prior to this 1929-1930-1931 stuff. I imagine that it must have been around 1907 or 1909. People couldn't hardly get five dollars for a bale of cotton. It started from all those boll weevil plagues that would eat up most of the crops.

——Skip James

Charlie Patton

Sees a little boll weevil keeps movin' in the . . . Lordie!
You can plant your cotton and you won't get a half a bale, Lordie.
Bo weevil, bo weevil, where's your native home? Lordie,
"A-Louisiana raised in Texas, least is where I was bred and born," Lordie.
Well, I saw the bo weevil, Lord, a-circle, Lord, in the air, Lordie,
The next time I seed him, Lord, he had his family there, Lordie.
Bo weevil left Texas, Lord, he bid me "fare ye well," Lordie,
(*Spoken:* Where you goin' now?)
"I'm goin' down the Mississippi, gonna give Louisiana hell," Lordie.
Bo weevil said to the farmer, "'Tain't got ticket fare," Lordie,
(*Spoken:* How is that, boy?)
Suck all the blossom and he leave your hedges square, Lordie,
The next time I seed you, you know you had your family there, Lordie.
Bo weevil meet his wife, "We can sit down on the hill," Lordie,
Bo weevil told his wife, "Let's trade this forty† in," Lordie,
Bo weevil told his wife, says, "I believe I may go North," Lordie.
(*Spoken:* Hold on, I'm gonna tell all about that.)
"Let's leave Louisiana, we can go to Arkansas," Lordie.
Well, I saw the bo weevil, Lord, a-circle, Lord, in the air, Lordie,
Next time I seed him, Lord, he had his family there, Lordie.
Bo weevil told the farmer that "I 'tain't got ticket fare," Lordie,
Sucks all the blossom and leave your hedges square, Lordie.
Bo weevil, bo weevil, where your native home, Lordie?
"Most anywhere they raise cotton and corn," Lordie.
Bo weevil, bo weevil, "Oughta treat me fair," Lordie,
The next time I did you had your family there, Lordie.

*"Weevil" was so spelled on the original issue of this song by Paramount Records.
†*forty:* forty acres of land

Nappy Head Blues*

Medium fast

Bobby Grant

When you hear me walk - in' turn your lamp down, turn your lamp down, lamp down low. When you hear me walk - in', turn your lamp down low. When you hear me walk - in', turn your lamp down low. And turn it so your man'll nev - er know.

When you hear me walkin', turn your lamp down, turn your lamp down, lamp down low,
When you hear me walkin', turn your lamp down low. (twice)
And turn it so your man'll never know.

Gonna buy me a bed, and it shine like a mornin', shine like a mornin', a mornin' star,†
I'm gonna buy me a bed and it shine like a mornin' star. (twice)
When I gets to bed, it rock like a Cadillac car.

Your head is nappy, feets so mamley, feets so mamley, mamlish long,
Your head is nappy, your feets so mamlish long. (twice)
And you like a turkey comin' through the mamlish corn.

I done told you I loved you, what more can I, what more can I, can I do?
I done told you I loved you, what more can I do? (twice)
Then you must a-want me to lay down and die for you.

*Nappy: kinky
†Unless Grant is referring to a brass bed, the comparison is far-fetched.

Salty Dog *

Mississippi John Hurt
Copyright © 1963 Wynwood Music Co. Inc.
All Rights Reserved   Used by Permission

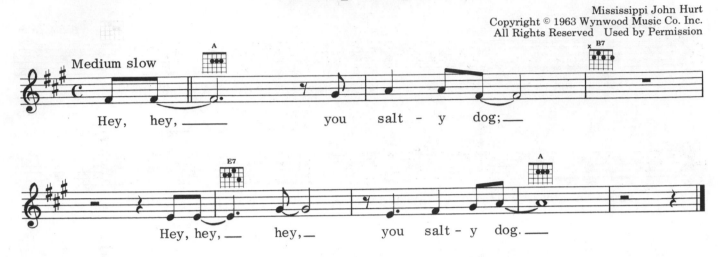

Medium slow

Hey,   hey, _____   you   salt - y   dog; _____

Hey, hey, ___   hey, ___   you   salt - y   dog. _____

Spoken:
"Salty Dog."

Hey-hey, you salty dog,
Hey-hey-hey, you salty dog.

Said, the little fish, big fish swimmin'
    in the water,
Come back, man, and gimme my quarter.
Hey-hey-hey, you salty dog.

Said, the scaredest I ever was in my life,
Uncle Bud like to caught me kissin' his wife.
Hey-hey, you salty dog.

Third verse hummed.

Says, God made woman, made 'em mighty funny,
The lips 'round her mouth, just as sweet
    as any honey.
Hey-hey, you salty dog.

Hey-hey, you salty dog,
Hey-hey-hey, you salty dog.

(*Spoken:* Well . . !)
Well, little fish, big fish swimmin' in the water,
Come back here, man, gimme my quarter.
Hey-hey-hey, you salty dog.

*When asked the meaning of "salty dog," Hurt sheepishly replied,
  "To tell you the truth, I never thought about it."

Motherless Child Blues

My mother told me just before she died, (four times)

"Oh daughter, daughter, please don't be like me,
Oh daughter, oh daughter, please don't be like me, (twice)
You'll fall in love with every man you see."

But I did not listen to what my mother said,
But I did not listen what my mother said, (twice)
That's the reason why I'm driftin' here in Hattiesburg.

Baby, now she's dead, six feet in the ground,
Baby, now she's dead, she's six feet in the ground, (twice)
And I'm a child* and I am driftin' around.

Do you remember the day, baby, you drove me from your door? (twice)
Do you remember the day you drove me from your door?
"Go away from here, woman, and don't come here no more."

I walked away and I wring my hands and cryin', (three times)
Didn't have no blues but I couldn't keep tarryin' around.

*As it was commonly used in Negro speech, "child" simply specified a
person as opposed to a thing. It is used by Robert Johnson and other
blues artists as an affectionate form of address.

Bob McKinney*

Moderately fast

Henry Thomas

Went down on John - son Street,— Bob Mc - Kin - ney came pass - in' by.— Goin' down there on John - son Street,— make trou - ble in their lives. Was - n't he "bad?"———— Ju - st was - n't he "bad?"

Went down on Johnson Street, Bob McKinney come passin' by,
Goin' down there on Johnson Street, make trouble in their lives.
Wasn't he *bad?* Just wasn't he *bad?*

Bobby said to Marg'et, "Come to me, I say,
If you don't come in a hurry, I put a thirty-eight through your head."
Wasn't he *bad?* Just wasn't he *bad?*

Bobby said to Ben Ferris, "I'm bound to take your life,
You've caused trouble between me and my wife."
Wasn't he *bad?* Just wasn't he *bad?*

Bobby said to the high sheriff, "Needn't think I'm going to run,
If I had another load, me and you have some fun."
Wasn't he *bad?* Just wasn't he *bad?*

Oh, my babe, take me back. Why in the world don't take me back?
One of these mornin', won't be long, you gonna call me, I'll be gone.
She turned around, two or three times, begged my babe, "Take me back,
Take me back, take me back," begged my babe, "take me back."

Oh, make me a pallet on your floor,
Hey, make me one pallet on your floor,
Oh, make a pallet on your floor.
Won't you make it so your man'll never know?

Hey, make it so your man never know,
Hey, make it so your man never know,
Aw make a pallet, on your . . .
Won't you make it so your man never know?

*The latter part of this medley is made up of traditional folk tunes: "Take
Me Back" (also called "Beggin' Back"), "Pallet on the Floor," and an identical melody, "Lookin' for the Bully of This Town."

Yes, I'm lookin' for that bully lay me down,
Hey, I'm lookin' for that bully lay me down,
I'm lookin' for that bully, that bully can't be . . .
Yes, I'm lookin' for that bully laid me down.

Hey, I'm lookin' for that bully lay me down,
Hey, I'm lookin' for the bully lay me down,
I'm lookin' for that bully, an' the bully can't be found.
I'm lookin' for that bully lay me down.

M & O Blues*

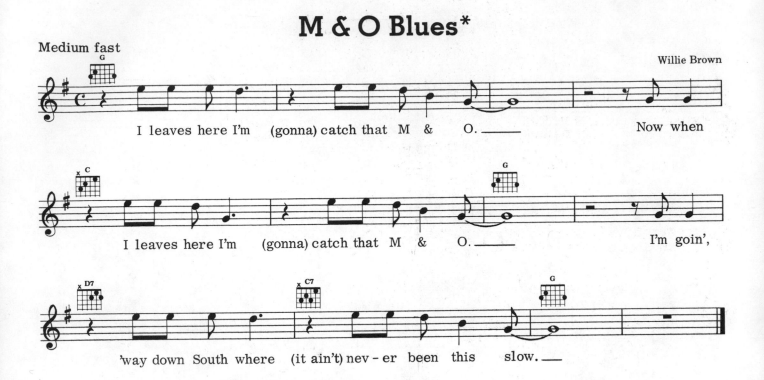

I leaves here I'm (gonna) catch that M&O,
Now, when I leaves here I'm (gonna) catch that M&O,
I'm goin' way down South where (it ain't) never been this slow.

'Cause I had a notion, Lord, and I believe I will,
'Cause I had a notion, Lord, and I believe I will,
I'm gonna build me a mansion out on Decatur† hill.

Now, it's all o' you men, oughta be 'shamed of yourself,
And it's all o' you men, oughta be 'shamed of yourself,
Goin' 'round here swearin' 'fore God you got a poor woman by yourself.‡

I started to kill my woman till she laid down 'cross the bed,
I started to kill my woman till, laid down 'cross the bed,
And she looked so ambitious** till I took back everything I said.

And I asked her, "How 'bout it?" Lord, and she said, "All right."
And I asked her, "How 'bout it?" Lord, and she said, "All right."
But she never showed up at the shack last night,
And she . . .

*M&O: The Mobile and Ohio Railroad.
†Perhaps the allusion is to Decatur, Mississippi.
‡This stanza probably remarks on the imagined infidelity of women.
**Ambitious: angry, in backwoods speech.

Louis Collins*

Mississippi John Hurt
Copyright © 1963 Wynwood Music Co. Inc.
All Rights Reserved   Used by Permission

Mrs. Col - lins weeped, Mrs. Col - lins moaned _ to see her son Lou - is leav - in' home. The an - gels laid him a - way.

Mrs. Collins weeped, Mrs. Collins moaned
To see her son Louis leavin' home.
The angels laid him away.

The angels laid him away,
They laid him six feet under the clay.
The angels laid him away.

Mrs. Collins weeped, Mrs. Collins moaned
To see her son Louis leavin' home.
The angels laid him away.

Oh, Bob shot once and Louis shot, too, [two]
Shot poor Collins, shot him through
    and through.
The angels laid him away.

Oh, kind friends, oh, ain't it hard?
To see poor Louis in a new graveyard.
The angels laid him away.

The angels laid him away,
They laid him six feet under the clay.
The angels laid him away.

Oh, when they heard that Louis was dead,
All the people, they dressed in red.
The angels laid him away.

The angels laid him away,
They laid him six feet under the clay.
The angels laid him away.

Mrs. Collins weeped, Mrs. Collins moaned
To see her son Louis leavin' home.
The angels laid him away.

The angels laid him away,
They laid him six feet under the clay.
The angels laid him away.

*According to Hurt, this song (his own composition) was based on
 a true episode.

Spike Driver Blues

Mississippi John Hurt

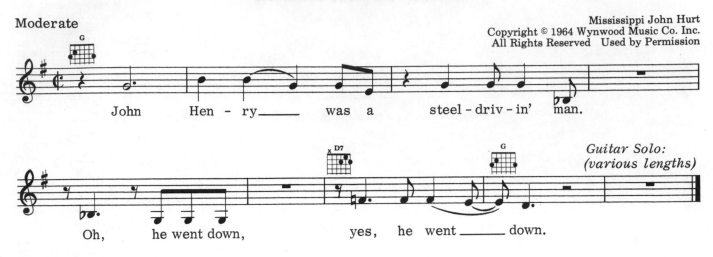

John Henry was a steel-drivin' man,
Oh, he went down, yes, he went down.

John Henry, he had a little wife,
Name was Polly Anne, name was Polly Anne.

John Henry took sick in the bed,
She drove steel like a man, drove steel
    like a man.

I walked here all the way from east Colorado,
Baby, that's my home, honey, that's my home.

You can take this hammer and carry it
    to my captain,
Oh, tell him I'm gone, won't you tell him
    I'm gone?

John Henry, he left his hammer
Layin' 'side the road, layin' 'side the road.

John Henry, he left his hammer,
All painted in red, all painted in red.

You just take this hammer and carry it
    to my captain,
Oh, tell him I'm gone, won't you tell him
    I'm gone?

Long Train Blues

Robert Wilkins

She walked down the yard, caught the longest train she seen, (twice)
Said she'd ride and ride "till the blues wear offa me."

It's two bullyin' freight trains runnin' side by side, (twice)
They done stole my rider and I guess they're satisfied.

They rode in the Delta, kept on easin' by, (twice)
Know I feel just like she said her last good-bye.

Friend, she won't write, she won't telephone, (twice)
Makes me believe to my soul my rider calls that "gone."*

But if I had wings, friend, like Noah's dove,
Friend, if I had wings, friend, like Noah's dove,
I would raise and fly, God knows, where my lover was.

I laid down at night, I can't sleep at all, (twice)
Awful lyin' there wondering if someone rollin' in her arms.

Laid my head on my pillow, friends, it be's too high, (twice)
Taken down with the (devil?), I'm gettin' sick and 'bout to die.

*The sham departure is reflected in an old Negro proverb, "Every
   good-bye ain't 'gone.'"

Little Woman You're So Sweet

Blind Boy Fuller
© Copyright 1944 J. Baxter Long
All Rights Reserved   Used by Permission

Hey mama, hey gal, don't you hear me callin' you?
You're so sweet, so sweet, my baby, so sweet.

Says, I love my baby, love her to her bone,
I hate to see my sweet sugar go home.
She's so sweet, so sweet, my little woman, so sweet.

See my baby comin', don't get so smart,
I'll cut your liver, then I will plug your heart.
You're so sweet, so sweet, so sweet, my little baby, so sweet.

Spoken:
Call again, boy!

Hey mama, yeah gal, don't you hear Blind Boy Fuller callin' you?
She's so sweet, yeah sweet, yeah sweet, my little woman, so sweet.

Spoken:
Play it, now

Hey mama, yeah gal, don't you hear me callin' you?
She's so sweet, so sweet, my little woman, so sweet.

Woman I love, she done gone back home,
When I think I'm treatin' her right I must be doin' wrong.
She's so sweet, so sweet, my little woman, so sweet.

I'll make a million trips where I would rather to be,
But the woman I love is sweeter than anything in this world to me.
She's so sweet, so sweet, my little woman, so sweet

Hey mama, hey gal, don't you hear Blind Boy Fuller callin' you?
You're so sweet, so sweet, yeah sweet, my little woman, so sweet.

Little Cow And Calf Is Gonna Die Blues *

Skip James
Copyright © 1965 Wynwood Music Co. Inc.
All Rights Reserved   Used by Permission

Hey,   hey, hey, hey, hey, __   hey, hey, hey, __   hey,   Hey,
hey, hey, hey, hey, __   hey,   hey, hey,   hey...   And ev-er-
y cow and calf, __   I be-lieve was   born   to   die. ____

Hey hey-hey-hey-hey, hey hey hey hey hey,
Hey hey-hey-hey-hey, hey hey hey hey . . .
And every cow and calf, I believe was
   born to die.

I'm a-milk my heifer, milk her in a churn,
I'll milk my heifer, I'll milk her in a churn,
If you see my rider, tell her it 'tain't
   a darn thing doin'.†

I wringed my hands, baby, and I wanted
   to scream,
I wringed my hands, honey, and I wanted
   to scream,
And when I woke up I thought it was
   all a dream.

Hey hey-hey-hey-hey, hey hey hey hey,
Hey hey-hey-hey-hey, hey hey hey hey . . .
And every cow and calf, she was born to die.

Hey hey-hey, I ain't gonna be here long,
Hey-hey-hey, pretty mama, I ain't gonna
   be here long,
That's the reason why you hear me singin'
   my old lonesome song.

Hey, hey-hey-hey-hey-hey, hey hey hey hey,
Hey hey-hey-hey-hey, hey hey hey hey hey,
And every cow's calf, honey, got to be dyin'.

I walked the levee from end to end,
I walked the levee, honey, from end to end,
I was just tryin' to find—my calf—again.

I'm feelin' back to my used-to . . .
I feel a notion, back to my used-to-be,
I have a pretty mama, she don't care for me.

*Although women are clearly represented by the expressions "heifer" and "calf" in the second and seventh verses, James described this song as the product of boyhood experiences tending his grandmother's cattle, whose waywardness drove him to distraction.

†Here James asks the listener to conceal his infidelity to his "rider."

Ain't You Sorry?

Mance Lipscomb
Copyright © 1970 Tradition Music Co.
All Rights Reserved   Used by Permission

Ain't you sorry to your heart?
Best o' friend, you know, they got to part.
Ain't you sorry, sorry that you did me wrong?

Now, me and my girl had a fallin' out,
Bet you don't know what was about.
She's sorry, sorry that you did me wrong.

Now, go on girl, you needn't flirt,
I know you done tore your underskirt.*
Ain't you sorry, sorry to your heart?

Well, I'm going up North, 'tain't goin' to stay,
Got a girl, chances gonna pay my way.
Ain't you sorry, sorry to your heart?

Ain't you sorry, sorry to your heart?
But the best o' friend, you know, got to part.
Ain't you sorry, sorry you did me wrong?

*This line is figurative. "To tear one's drawers," a fashionable
black expression of the twenties, is to make a spectacle of oneself.

Last Fair Deal Gone Down

Robert Johnson

It's the last fair deal gone down,
Last fair deal gone down,
It's the last fair deal gone down, good Lord,
On the Gulfport Island Road.*

An' Ida Bell, don't cry this time,
Ida Bell, don't cry this time,
If you cry about a nickel, you'll die
    about a dime,
She would cry, but the money, it ain't mine.

I like the way you do,
I love the way you do,
I love the way you do, good Lord,
On this Gulfport Island Road.

My Captain's so mean on me,
My Captain's so mean on me,
My Captain's so mean on, good Lord,
On this Gulfport Island Road.

That Camp A, B and C,
That Camp A, B and C,
That gal A, B and C, good Lord,
On that Gulfport Island Road.

Aw, this last fair deal gone down,
This the last fair deal gone down,
This the last fair deal gone down, good Lord,
On this Gulfport Island Road.

I'm workin' my way back home,
I'm workin' my way back home,
I'm workin' my way back home, good Lord,
On this Gulfport Island Road.

An' that thing† don't keep a-ringin' so soon,‡
That thing don't keep ringin' so soon,
An' that thing don't keep a-ringin' so soon,
    good Lord,
On that Gulf 'n' Port Island Road.

*Gulfport Island Road: Probably a construction or maintenance
  camp of the now defunct Gulf and Ship Island Railroad of Gulfport, Mississippi.
†that thing: probably a bell used to summon workers.
‡In blues, "soon" usually means early, e.g., soon this morning.

Banty Rooster Blues*

Charlie Patton

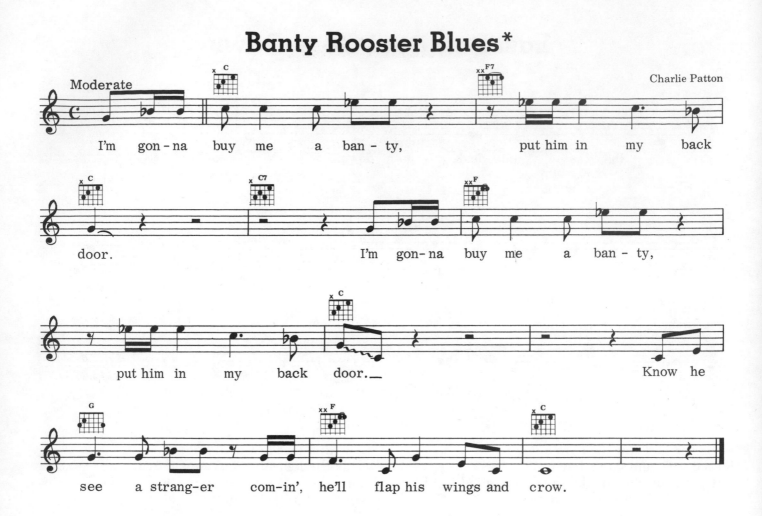

I'm gonna buy me a banty, put him in my back door, (twice)
Know he see a stranger comin', he'll flap his wings and crow.

What you want with a rooster, he won't crow 'fore day? (twice)
What you want with a man when he won't do nothin' he say?

What you want with a hen won't cackle when she lay? (twice)
What you want with a woman when she won't do nothin' I say?

Aw, take my picture, hang it up in Jackson Wall,† (twice)
If anybody asks you, "What's about it?" Tell 'em, "That's all, that's all."

My hook in the water and my cork's on top, (twice)
How can I lose, Lord, with the help of God?

I know my dog anywhere I hear him bark, (twice)
I can tell my rider if I feel her in the dark.

*Assuming that they are sequential, the first three couplets of this
  song would seem to depict a cuckold, with the second and third
  verses given over to his rejoinders to a skeptical wife and rival.
†Jackson Wall is presumably a barrelhouse. It has been reported
  that Mississippi barrelhouses of the twenties often featured pictures
  of local blues attractions.

Preachin' Blues

Son House

Oh, I'm gonna get me a religion, I'm gonna join the Baptist Church,
Oh, I'm gonna get me a religion, I'm gonna join the Baptist Church,
I'm gonna be a Baptist preacher, and I sure won't have to work.

Oh, I'm a-preach these blues, and I, I want everybody to shout,
. . . I want everybody to shout,
I'm gonna do like a prisoner, I'm gonna roll* my time on out.

Oh, I went in my room, I bowed down to pray,
Oh, I went in my room, I bowed down to pray,
Till the blues come along, and they blowed my spirit† away.

Oh, I'd-a had religion, Lord, this very day,
Oh, I'd-a had religion, Lord, this very day,
But the womens and whiskey, well, they would not set me free.

Oh, I wish I had me a heaven of my own,
(*Spoken:* Great God Almighty!)
Hey, a heaven of my own,
Till I'd give all my women a long, long, happy home.

Hey, I love my baby, just like I love myself,
Oh, just like I love myself,
Well, if she don't have me, she won't have nobody else.

roll: work
†*spirit:* religious spirit

Long Tall Girl Got Stuck On Me

Mance Lipscomb

Well, a long tall girl got stuck on me,
Well, a long tall girl got stuck on me.

I'm goin', don't you wanna go?
Well, I'm goin' where I never have been before.

And late last night, 'bout twelve,
Was late last night, just 'bout twelve,

Thought I heard my baby call my name,
Well, I thought I heard that woman call
      my name.

Lord, I'm goin' to hole in the ground,
Well, I'm going to the hole deep in the ground.

Baby, if you don't want me why'n't you say so?
Give me down my clothes and I will go.

Good-bye, babe, baby good-bye.
Honey, bye-bye baby, bye-bye-bye.

'Morrow may be my trial day,
What in the world is the judge gonna say?

Tell me, where you stay last night?
Ain't none of my business but I know
      it ain't right.

Kindhearted Woman Blues

Robert Johnson

I got a kindhearted woman, do anything (in) this world for me,
I got a kindhearted woman, do anything (in) this world for me,
But these evilhearted women, man, they will not let me be.

I love my baby, my baby don't love me,
I love my baby, my baby don't love me,
But I really love that woman, can't stand to leave her be.

There ain't but the one thing makes Mister Johnson drink,
Ask whoever how you treat me, baby, I begin to think.
Oh, babe, my life don't feel the same,
You breaks my heart when you call Mister So-and-So's name.

She's a kindhearted woman, she studies evil all the time,
She's a kindhearted woman, she studies evil all the time,
You wish to kill me, else to have it on your mind.

Casey Jones

Traditional, Arranged by Furry Lewis
Copyright © 1969 Uncle Doris Music, Ltd. (United Kingdom)
65 Parkway, London, N.W.1 7PP. U.S.A. controlled by
Uncle Doris Music, Inc. 165 West 74th Street, New York 10023

Medium fast

I woke up____ this morn-in' was a show-er of rain.____ A-round the curve_ was a pass-en-ger train._ Un-der the bot-tom was a Ho-bo John,_ He's a good old ho-bo but he's dead and gone, Dead and gone. Well, there was_

I woke up this mornin', was a shower of rain,
Around the curve was a passenger train.
Under the bottom was a Hobo John,
He's a good old hobo, but he's dead and gone,
Dead and gone.

Well, there was a woman named Miss Alice Fry,
Say, "I'm gonna ride with old Casey or die.
I ain't good-lookin' but I takes my time,
I'm a ramblin' woman, I got a ramblin' mind,
Got a ramblin' mind."

Now, Mister Casey said just before he died,
There one more road he would like to ride.
Fireman asked Case, "What road is he?"
"That's the Southern Pacific and the Santa Fe,
The Santa Fe, boy.
That Southern Pacific and the Santa Fe."

Well, I'm gonna leave Memphis to spread the news,
The Memphis women don't wear no shoes.
I got it written in the back of my shirt,
"I'm a natural-born eastman,* I don't have to work."
I don't have to work.
I'm a natural-born eastman, I don't have to work.

When I sold my gin, I sold it straight,
The police run me to my woman's gate.
She come to the door, she nod her head,
Say, "Furry, you're welcome to my foldin' bed,
My foldin' bed.
Furry, you're welcome to my foldin' bed."

Mister Casey run his engine in a mighty good place,
Number Four stabbed him right in the face.
The dicks told Casey, "You must leave town."
I believe to my soul I'm Alabama bound,
Alabama bound.
I believe to my soul I'm Alabama bound.

Now, if you wanna go to heaven when you d-i-e,
Put on your collar and a t-i-e.
If you wanna scare a rabbit outta l-o-g,
Just make a little stump like a d-o-g.
I'm on the road again.

*eastman: a man living on the earnings of a woman.

Spoonful Blues

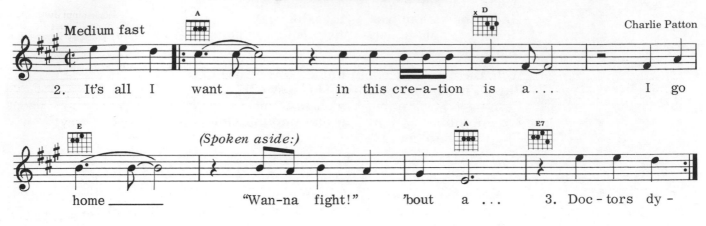

Charlie Patton

2. It's all I want _____ in this cre-a-tion is a . . . I go

home _____ *(Spoken aside:)* "Wan-na fight!" 'bout a . . . 3. Doc-tors dy-

Spoken:
I'm about to go to jail about this spoonful.

In all a spoon', 'bout that spoon',
The women goin' crazy every day in their life 'bout a . . .

It's all I want in this creation is a . . .
I go home (*spoken:* wanna fight!) 'bout a . . .

Doctors dyin' (*spoken:* way in Hot Springs!) just 'bout a . . .
These women goin' crazy every day in their life 'bout a . . .

Would you kill a man dead? (*spoken:* Yes I will!) just 'bout a . . .
Oh babe, I'm a fool about my . . .

(*Spoken:* Don't take me long!) to get my . . .
Hey baby, you know I need my . . .

It's mens on Parchman (*spoken:* done lifetime) just 'bout a . . .
Hey baby, (*spoken:* You know I ain't long) 'bout my . . .

It's all I want (*spoken:* honey, in this creation) is a . . .
I go to bed, get up and wanna fight 'bout a . . .

(*Spoken:* Lookey here, baby, would you slap me? Yes I will!) just 'bout a . . .
Hey baby, (*spoken:* you know I'm a fool a-) 'bout my . . .

Would you kill a man? (*spoken:* Yes I would, you know I'd kill him) just 'bout a . . .
Most every man (*spoken:* that you see is) fool 'bout his . . .

(*Spoken:* You know baby, I need) that ol' . . .
Hey baby, (*spoken:* I wanna hit the judge 'bout a) 'bout a . . .

(*Spoken:* Baby, you gonna quit me? Yeah honey!) just 'bout a . . .
It's all I want, baby, this creation is a . . .

(*Spoken:* Lookey here, baby, I'm leavin' town!) just 'bout a . . .
Hey baby, (*Spoken:* you know I need) that ol' . . .

(*Spoken:* Don't make me mad, baby!) 'cause I want my . . .
Hey baby, I'm a fool 'bout that . . .

(*Spoken:* Lookey here, honey!) I need that . . .
Most every man leaves without a . . .

Sundays' mean (*spoken:* I know they are) 'bout a . . .
Hey baby, (*spoken:* I'm sneakin' around here) and ain't got me no . . .
Oh, that spoon', hey baby, you know I need my . . .

Nobody's Dirty Business

Mississippi John Hurt
Copyright © 1964 Wynwood Music Co. Inc.
All Rights Reserved   Used by Permission

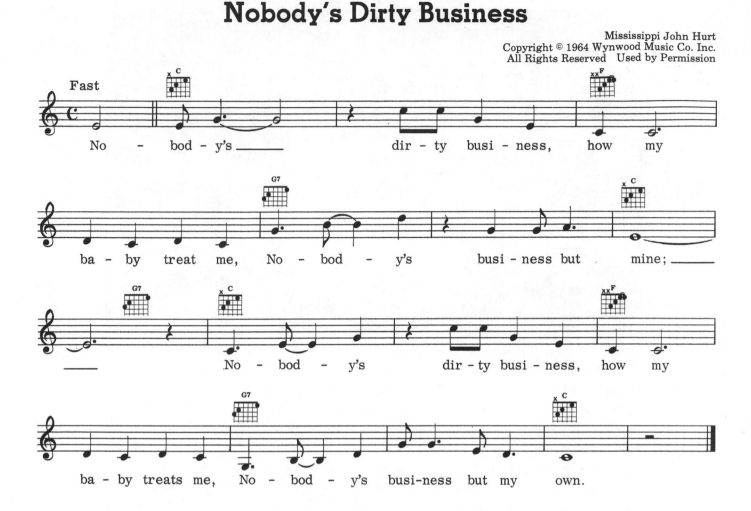

Nobody's dirty business how my baby treat me,
Nobody's business but mine.
Nobody's dirty business how my baby treat me,
Nobody's business but my own.

Sometimes my baby gets boozy, then again she tries to rule me,
Nobody's business but mine.
Nobody's dirty business how my baby treat me,
Nobody's business but my own.
(*Spoken:* That's all right, just let her rule me.)

Say, baby, did you get that letter? "If you take me back I'll treat you better."
Nobody's business but mine.
Nobody's dirty business how my baby treats me,
Nobody's business but my own.

I'm goin' back to Pensacola, gonna buy my baby a money (muller?)*
Nobody's business but mine.
Nobody's dirty business how my baby treat me,
Nobody's business but my own.

Nobody's . . .
Nobody's business but mine.
Nobody's dirty business how my baby treat me,
Nobody's business but my own.

*muller: a grinding tool

191

You Can't Keep No Brown

Bo' Weevil Jackson

Medium

I woke up this morn-in' ma-ma, blues all __ a-round my bed.

Soon this morn-in' ma-ma, blues all a-round my__ bed.

Think-in' 'bout the kind word that my ma-ma had said.

I woke up this mornin', mama, blues all around my bed,
Soon this mornin', mama, blues all around my bed,
Thinkin' 'bout the kind word that my mama had said.

Now, my mama is dead, so is my daddy, too,
Now, my mama's dead, so is my daddy, too,
That's the reason I tried so hard to get along with you.

Now, where there ain't no lovin', ain't no gettin' along,
Where there ain't no lovin', sure ain't no gettin' along,
'Cause you'll have more trouble, honey, than all the day is long.

So many days I stoled away and cried,
So many days I stoled away and cried,
Poor boy has been mistreated an' I can't be satisfied.

I'm gonna write a letter, mail it in the air,
I'm gonna write a letter, gonna mail it in the air,
Because the March wind blow, it blow news everywhere.

Girl, I'm goin' up the country, won't be very long,
Girl, I'm goin' up the country, won't be very long,
Little gal, you can count the days that I'm gone.

Papa's in a hurry, don't have to fight!
I gotta get hitched up, the saddle is too light.
I'm crazy about my jane, tell the world that I do,
'Cause I'm goin' where they sing long-distance blues.

Got a little fair brownie keep ballin' the jack,*
Her screamin' and fightin'll get me snatchin' it back.
I wanna see my jane, tell the world that I do,
'Cause I'm goin' where they sing long-distance blues.

*ballin' the jack: a dance popular among blacks which probably
  gave rise to the 1913 song hit of the same name. In blues songs
  the reference to it may have served as shorthand for wild behavior
  in general, as did references to the shimmy, which ballin' the jack
  is said to resemble.

Hoist Your Window and Let Your Curtain Down

Joe Callicott
Copyright © 1969 Uncle Doris Music, Ltd. (United Kingdom)
65 Parkway, London, N.W.1 7PP.—U.S.A. controlled by
Uncle Doris Music, Inc. 165 West 74th Street, New York 10023
All Rights Reserved   Used by Permission

Spoken: Go on. Go on, now!

Goin' away, won't be worried long,*
Lord, I'm worried, baby, won't be worried long,
I'm worried, won't be worried . . .

Oh, hurry . . . soon,
Well now, hurry, hurry, it won't be so soon,
Some other joker sure gonna take your room.

Go hoist your . . . let your curtain down,
Gonna hoist your window, let your
        curtain down,
I ain't so sleepy, baby, feel like lyin' . . .

Oh, some old day, Lordie Lord,
. . . day you gonna hunt me soon,
Well, some old day you gonna hunt me soon.

When you see me singin' the worried song,
Now, when you see me sittin' down, singin'
        the worried song,
Oughta know by that, poor Joe ain't here
        for long.

Gonna hoist your . . . let your curtain down,
Gonna hoist your window, let your
        curtain down,
Well, I ain't so sleepy, feel like lyin' down.

I'm a poor boy . . . Lordie Lord,
I'm a poor boy, a poor boy, out in the
        world some . . .
I'm a poor boy, a poor boy, out in the
        world somewhere.

Well, the woman I had had, she walked away
        from me,
Well, the woman I had walked away from me,
Well, put me in the alley, where I want to be.

Say, your hair ain't . . . and your eyes
        ain't blue,
(*Spoken:* Tellin' about me, baby!)
Well, your hair ain't curly and your eyes
        ain't blue,
Says, I got one sister, what I want with you?

*The emphasis of the first line of each verse is less on the words
than on falsetto singing; hence the broken delivery of some lines.
We have omitted the final verse, which is partly instrumentalized
and is unrhymed.

Corrinne, Corrinna

Mississippi John Hurt

Moderate

I left Cor - in - a   way a-cross_ the sea.

Lord, I left__ Cor - in - a   way a-cross the

sea.   She would-n't write me no let - ter,

she don't ca - re for me.__   Oh,___   Cor -

I left Corinna way across the sea,
Lord, I left Corinna way across the sea,
She wouldn't write me no letter, she don't
      care for me.

Oh Corinne, where you been so long?
Oh Corinna, where you been so long?

Corinna, Corinne, where'd you stay last night?
Oh Corinna, where'd you stay last night?
Come in this mornin', clothes ain't
      fittin' you right.

Oh Corinne, where you been so long?
Oh Corinna, where you been so long?

That's No Way To Get Along

Robert Wilkins

I'm goin' home, friends, sit down and tell my, my mama,
Friends, sit down and tell my ma.
I'm goin' home, sit down and tell my ma (twice)
That that's no way to get along.

These low-down women, mama, they treated your, aw, poor son wrong,
Mama, treated me wrong.
These low-down women, mama, treated your poor son wrong. (twice)
And that's no way for him to get along.

They treated me like my poor heart was made of a rock or stone,
Mama, made of a rock or stone.
Treated me like my poor heart was made of a rock or stone. (twice)
And that's no way for me to get along.

You know, that was enough, mama, to make your son wished he's dead and gone,
Mama, wished I's dead and gone.
That is enough to make your son, mama, wished he's dead and gone. (twice)
'Cause that's no way for him to get along.

I stood on the roadside, I cried alone, all by myself,
I cried alone by myself.
I stood on the roadside and cried alone by myself. (twice)
Cryin', "That's no way for me to get along."

I's wantin' some train to come along and take me away from here,
Friends, take me 'way from here.
Some train to come along and take me away from here. (twice)
And that's no way for me to get along.

Roberta

Lil' Son Jackson
Copyright © 1968 Tradition Music Co.
All Rights Reserved   Used by Permission

Yon come Roberta with a hundred dollars in her hand,
Well, come Roberta with a hundred dollars in her hand,
She said, "Good mornin', Judge, you know I come to get my man."

Well now, the judge turn around an' he begin to chew his cud,
Well now, the judge turn around, boys, begin to chew his cud,
He said, "A hundred, Roberta, won't do your man no good."

Did thirty days in jail with my back turned to the wall,
Thirty days in jail with my back turned to the wall,
Well, I taken my Christmas, baby, in my overall.

Well, an' they brought me coffee, oh man, they brought me tea,
Well, they brought me coffee, don't you know they brought me tea?
Well, honey, they brought me everything, oh Lord, but the jailhouse key.

I Would If I Could

Sam Hopkins

Gon-na take my baby, (goin') to the pic-ture show.

I'm gon-na take my baby, (we goin') to the pic-ture show.

I gon-na make ev-'ry-bod-y get back 'cause we got to sit in the front row.

Gonna take my baby, goin' to the picture show,
I'm gonna take my baby, we goin' to the picture show.
I'm gonna make everybody get back, 'cause we got to sit in the front row.

I know they gonna say I'm crazy, gonna call poor Lightnin' insane,
They gonna call me crazy, they gonna say poor Lightnin's insane.
Ain't but one picture I wanna see, and that's old "Jesse James."

I'm gonna tell 'em I would if I could, I'm gonna tell 'em I would if I could,
But I just can't shoot that good.
But I'm still gonna tell 'em ol' Lightnin' would if I could.

Spoken:
You know Jesse James' the baddest man I ever saw. He walked
in the lion's den, he slapped the he-lion, he knocked the she-
lion's jaw, Lord have mercy. I would if I could, but I just can't
shoot that good. Yeah.

Thousand Woman Blues

Blind Boy Fuller
© Copyright 1944, J. Baxter Long
All Rights Reserved   Used by Permission

I ain't   nev - er lov - ed   but a

thou - sand wom - en   in _____ my   life.   O - o - oh   Lord,____

____ but a   thou - sand   wom - ens   in   my   life. ____

I ain't never loved but a thousand women
    in my life,
Oh Lord, but a thousand womens in my life.

Now, the love I have for you, woman, God knows
    it sure is strong,
Oh Lord, I say, God knows it sure is strong.

Then if you love me now, woman, then you won't
    do nothin' wrong,
Hey Lord, and you won't do nothin' wrong.

Now my woman, please don't worry, baby, while
    I'm outta your town,
Hey Lord, I say, while I'm outta your town.

Now the love I have for you, mama, God knows
    it can't be turned around,
Hey, hey Lord, and it can't be turned around.

Now, my little woman, I said she's sweet as
    she can be,
Hey Lord, yes she's just as sweet as she can be.

An' every time I kiss her, then the cold
    chill run all over me,
Hey Lord, then the cold chill run over me.

Bull Frog Blues*

William Harris

5. I got the bull frog blues, ma - ma, I can't be sat - is —
I can't be sat - is — mam-lish 'fied! I got the bull frog blues now,
can't be sat - is - fied.____ Got the
bull frog blues an' I can't be sat - is - fied.____

Have you ever woke up with them bullfrogs on your, bullfrogs on your—I mean mind!?
Have you ever woke up, mama, bullfrog on your mind?
Have you ever woke up with them bullfrogs on your mind?

Said it rained here, mama, sun shinin' in your, sun shinin' in your—I mean door!
It's gonna rain today, mama, sun shine in your door.
Gonna rain today, the sun is shinin' in your back door.

An' I'm gonna tell you this time, mama, I ain't gonna tell you no,
    ain't gonna tell you no—I mean more!
I'm gonna tell you this time, mama, ain't gonna tell you no more.
I'm gonna leave you, partner, an' I won't be back here no more.

I left you standin' here, buddy, in your back door, in your back door—bullfrog blues!
I left you here standin', mama, your back door . . .
I left you standin' here, in your back door cryin'.

I got the bullfrog blues, mama, I can't be satis—, I can't be satis—mamlish-fied!
I got the bullfrog blues, now, can't be satisfied.
Got the bullfrog blues, an' I can't be satisfied.

Have you ever dreamed lucky, woke up cold in, woke up cold in—I mean hand!?
Have you ever dream lucky, woke up cold in hand?
Have you ever dream lucky, woke up cold in hand?

*The idea of "bullfrog blues" may have been suggested by the bullfrog hop, a twenties'
  dance.

I'm gonna tell you, buddy, what a Chinaman told a, Chinaman told a—I mean a Jew!
I'm gonna tell you what a Chinaman told a Jew,
"If you don't liketed me, why I sure God don't like you."

Hey, lookey here, partner, see what you done to, see what you done to—I mean me!?
Lookey here, partner, see what you done to me?
Hey, lookey here, partner, see what you done to me?

Hey, the sun gonna shine in my back door some, my back door some—I say the day!
The sun gonna shine in my back door some day.
Hey, the sun gonna shine in my back door some day.

Rolling Stone

Robert Wilkins

Oh, the last time I seen her standing on the station cryin',
Oh, the last time I seen her, she's standing on the station cryin'.

Believe she told her friend, "Yon go that mind of mine,
Believe she told her friend, "Yon go that mind of mine.

"I don't mind him goin', he's gone and leave me here,
I don't mind him goin', he's gone and leave me here.

"Got to go back home, sleep all night by myself,
Got to go back home, sleepin' all night by myself."

Man, don't your house feel lonesome when your biscuit roller gone?
Man, don't your house feel lonesome when your biscuit roller's gone?

You stand in your back door and cry by yourself, alone,
You stand in your back door, cryin' by yourself, alone.

Cryin', "Ain't it enough to make a poor man wish he's dead and gone?"
Cryin', "Ain't it enough to make a poor man wished he's dead and gone?"

'Cause that woman he love, she's gone and left him alone,
'Cause that woman he love, she's gone and left him 'lone.

"Oh, looks like I ain't seen you in six long months today.
Oh, looks like I ain't seen her, six long months today."

Ain't it enough to make a poor man, great God, walk away?
Ain't it enough to make a poor man, great God, walk away?

Little Antoinette

Sam Hopkins
Copyright © 1971 Tradition Music Co.
All Rights Reserved   Used by Permission

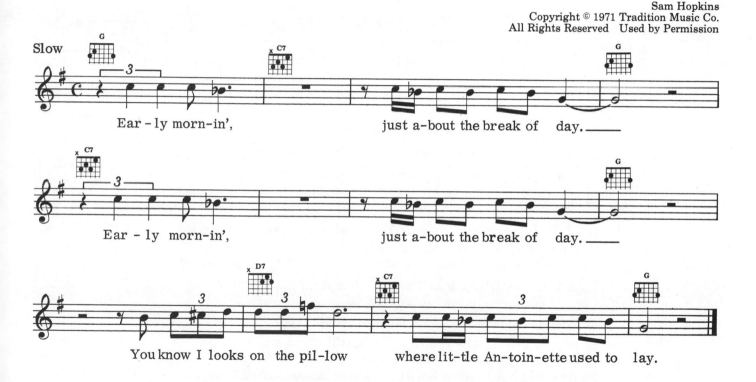

Early mornin', just about the break of day,
Early in the mornin', just about the break of day,
You know, I looks on the pillow
Where little Antoinette used to lay.

Felt to my pillow, yes, you know my pillow felt warm,
Felt to my pillow, oh Lord, and my pillow felt warm.
You know, you could tell about that dear friend,
Oh, Antoinette hadn't been very long gone.

She used to cook my breakfast, fix my table like you should,
She used to cook my breakfast, oh Lord, and fix my table like you should.
You know, when I sit down to eat my breakfast,
Lord, the meals she fixed me sure is good.

. . . She say I'd do it again if I could.

Dry Well Blues*

Charlie Patton

Way down in Lula,† hard livin' has done hit,
Way down in Lula, hard livin' has done hit,
Lord, your drought come an' caught us, an' parched up all the tree.

Aw, she stays over in Lula, bid that ol' town good-bye,
Stays in Lula, bidding you the town good-bye,
'Fore I would come to know the day, oh, the Lula well was gone dry.

Lord, there're citizens around Lula, aw, was doin' very well,
Citizens around Lula, aw, was doin' very well,
Now they're in hard luck together, 'cause rain don't pour nowhere.

I ain't got no money and I sure ain't got no hope,
Lord, I ain't got no money and I sure ain't got no hope,
... come in, furnished all the cotton and crops.

Boy, they tell me the country, Lord, it'll make you cry,
Lord, country, Lord, it'll make you cry,
Most anybody, Lord, hasn't any water in the bayou.‡

Lord, the Lula womens, Lord, puttin' Lula young mens down,
Lula 'men, oh, puttin' Lula men down,
Lord, you oughta been there, Lord, the womens all leavin' town.

*A pint of carbonated Lula water (bottled in 1930) will be awarded to the
first reader who decodes Patton's delivery of this song, which is so
garbled as to preclude a trustworthy transcription. Its topical significance
warrants its inclusion in this volume.
†At the time he recorded this work Patton lived in Lula, Mississippi.
‡If "bayou" is indeed the rhyme word of this verse, it is pronounced "by."

Candy Man Blues

Mississippi John Hurt
Copyright © 1963 Wynwood Music Co. Inc.
All Rights Reserved   Used by Permission

All you la-dies gath-er 'round, _ The good sweet can-dy-man's in _ town.   Can-dy-

man,   can-dy- man.

All you ladies, gather 'round,
The good, sweet candyman's in town,
Candyman, candyman!

He's got stick candy that's nine inches long,
He sells it faster than a hog can chew his corn,
Candyman, candyman!

All heard what sister Johnson said,
She always takes a candystick to bed,
Candyman, candyman!

Aw, his stick candy don't melt away,
It just gets better, so the ladies say,
Candyman, candyman!

Yes, can't stand close to the candyman,
He'll ease a stick of candy in your hand,
Candyman, candyman!

Yes, you and the candyman, you're gettin'
mighty sick, mm hmm . . .

Unh huh, oh yeah,
Oh yeah, yes, yes!

I say, you and the candyman, you're gettin'
mighty sick, mm hmm, mm hmm,
You must be stuck on the candyman's stick,
oh yeah, oh yeah.

Me And The Devil Blues

Robert Johnson

Early this mornin' when you knocked upon my door,
Early this mornin' when you knocked upon my door,
An' I said, "Hello, Satan, I believe it's time to go."

Me an' the devil, both walkin' side by side,
Me an' the devil was walkin' side by side,
I'm goin' to beat my woman until I get satisfied.

She said, "You don't see why"—that I will dog her 'round,
(*Spoken:* Now baby, you *know* you ain't doin' me right, now)
You say you don't see why that I would dog her 'round,
It musta be that old evil spirit so deep down in the ground.

You may bury my body down by the highway side,
(*Spoken:* Baby, I don't care where you bury my body when I'm dead and gone)
You may bury my body down by the highway side
So my old evil spirit can get a Greyhound bus an' ride.

Discography

All of the songs appearing in this book were transcribed from their original recordings in the 1920s or from the albums of some rediscovered bluesmen. Since no manuscripts exist of most of these songs, our lyrics for them are necessarily arbitrary. Although we have done everything within our power to make them accurate reflections of the original recordings, it should be remembered that the sequence of verses is rarely important in any blues performance.

The albums on which the material used in this book may be heard are listed below. Readers who are unable to obtain the blues reissues produced by small specialty labels can write directly to the companies themselves:

Yazoo and Blue Goose Records
54 King Street
New York City, New York 10014

Biograph and Historical Records
1601 East 21st Street
Brooklyn, New York 11210

Arhoolie Records
and Blues Classics Records
P.O. Box 9195
Berkeley, California 94719

Aberdeen Mississippi Blues, Booker "Bukka" White/ CBS 52629 | Realm Jazz Series
'Bout a Spoonful, Mance Lipscomb/ Arhoolie F.1001
Alabama Blues, Robert Wilkins/ Historical Records, ASC 5829-22
Ain't You Sorry?, Mance Lipscomb/ Arhoolie F.1033
All Night Long, Skip James/ Vanguard 79219, Biograph 12016, Melodeon 7321
At Home Blues, Sam Hopkins/ Arhoolie F.1034
Avalon Blues, Mississippi John Hurt/ Vanguard 19/20
Awful Fix Blues, Buddy Boy Hawkins/ Yazoo L.1004
Banty Rooster Blues, Charlie Patton/ Yazoo L.1020
Beer Drinkin' Women, B.K. Turner/ Arhoolie F.1017
Big Chief Blues, Furry Lewis/ Yazoo L.1002
Big Leg Blues, Mississippi John Hurt/ Yazoo L.1009
Bird Nest Bound, Charlie Patton/ Yazoo L.1020
Bob McKinney, Henry Thomas/ Origin of Jazz Library
Bud Russell Blues, Sam Hopkins/ Arhoolie F.1034
Bull Frog Blues, William Harris/ Origin of Jazz Library
Candyman, Mississippi John Hurt/ Vanguard 19032, Vanguard 19/20
Casey Jones, Furry Lewis/ Folkways — "An Anthology of American Folk Music," Blue Horizon 7-63228
Casey Jones, Mississippi John Hurt/ Melodeon Records
Catfish Blues, Skip James/ Vanguard 79273, Biograph 12016
Charlie James, Mance Lipscomb/ Arhoolie F.1023
Cherry Ball Blues, Skip James/ Yazoo L.1009, Vanguard 79219
Cocaine Done Killed My Baby, Mance Lipscomb/ Arhoolie F.1023
Coffee Blues, Mississippi John Hurt/ Vanguard 19/20, Vanguard 19032
Corrinne, Corrinna, Mississippi John Hurt/ Vanguard 19032
County Farm Blues, Son House/ XTRA 1080, Folkways Records
Crossroad Blues, Robert Johnson/ CBS 62456 Archive Series
Crow Jane, Skip James/ Vanguard 79219
Cypress Grove Blues, Skip James/ Vanguard 79219, Yazoo L.1001
Depot Blues, Son House/ XTRA 1080
Devil Got My Woman, Skip James/ Vanguard 79273, Melodeon 7321
Devil In The Lion's Den, Sam Collins/ Origin of Jazz Library #10
Dough Roller Blues, Joe Callicott/ Blue Horizon 7-63227
Down The Dirt Road, Charlie Patton/ Yazoo L.1020
Drunken Spree, Skip James/ Vanguard 79219, Biograph 12016
Dry Well Blues, Charlie Patton/ Yazoo L.1020
Fallin' Down Blues, Robert Wilkins/ Yazoo L.1002
Frankie, Mississippi John Hurt/ Folkways RF202, and Folkways— "An Anthology of American Folk Music"
From Four Until Late, Robert Johnson/ CBS 64102
Furry's Blues, Furry Lewis/ Blue Horizon 7-63210
Future Blues, Willie Brown/ Origin of Jazz Library #5
Get Away Blues, Robert Wilkins/ Origin of Jazz Library

Got The Blues, Can't Be Satisfied, Mississippi John Hurt/ Origin of Jazz Library #5, Vanguard 79248
Hambone Blues, Ed Bell/ Origin of Jazz Library
Hammer Blues, Charlie Patton/ Yazoo L.1020
Hard Time Killing Floor, Skip James/ Origin of Jazz Library #5, Vanguard 79219, Melodeon 7321
Hellhound On My Trail, Robert Johnson/ CBS 62456
High Sheriff Blues, Charlie Patton/ Yazoo L.1020
Hoist Your Window . . ., Joe Callicott/ Blue Horizon 7-63227
Hot Jelly Roll Blues, George Carter/ Yazoo L.1012
How Long Buck, Skip James/ Vanguard 79219
If I Had Possession Over My Judgement Day, Robert Johnson/ CBS 62456
If You Don't Want Me, Mississippi John Hurt/ Vanguard 19032
If You Haven't Any Hay, Skip James/ Origin of Jazz Library #5
I'll Go With Her Blues, Robert Wilkins/ Origin of Jazz Library
Illinois Blues, Skip James/ Vanguard 79273, Biograph 12016
I'm Satisfied, Mississippi John Hurt/ Vanguard 19032
I'm So Glad, Skip James/ Vanguard 79219
I Would If I Could, Sam Hopkins/ Arhoolie F.1034
Jinx Blues, Son House/ Herwin Records
Kindhearted Woman Blues, Robert Johnson/ CBS 62456, CBS 64102
Knocking Down Windows, Mance Lipscomb/ Arhoolie 1026
Last Fair Deal Gone Down, Robert Johnson/ CBS 62456
Lazy Blues, Mississippi John Hurt/ Vanguard 79248
Little Antoinette, Sam Hopkins/ Arhoolie 1034
Little Cow and Calf Is Gonna Die Blues, Skip James/ Vanguard 79273
Little Woman, You're So Sweet, Blind Boy Fuller/ Folkways 3585
Lonesome Atlanta Blues, Bobby Grant/ Yazoo L.1009
Long Tall Girl . . ., Mance Lipscomb/ Arhoolie F.1033
Long Train Blues, Robert Wilkins/ Historical Records, ASC5829-2
Lost Lover Blues, Blind Boy Fuller/ Phillips Records
Louis Collins, Mississippi John Hurt/ Origin of Jazz Library #5, Vanguard 19032
Low Down Dirty Dog Blues, Son House/ XTRA 1080
M & O Blues, Willie Brown/ Origin of Jazz Library #5
Married Woman Blues, Joe Callicott/ Blue Horizon 7-63227
Me And The Devil Blues, Robert Johnson/ CBS 62456
Mississippi Bo Weavil, Charlie Patton/ Yazoo L.1020
Mississippi Moan, The Mississippi Moaner/ Yazoo L.1009
Moon Going Down, Charlie Patton/ Yazoo L.1020
Motherless Child Blues, Elvie Thomas/ Origin of Jazz Library, The Country Girls
My Black Mama, Son House/ Origin of Jazz Library #2
My Creole Belle, Mississippi John Hurt/ Vanguard 19/20
My Mother Died, Booker "Bukka" White/ Blue Horizon 7-63210
Nappy Head Blues, Bobby Grant/ Yazoo L.1001

Nashville Stonewall Blues, Robert Wilkins/ Historical Records
ASC5829-22
Nobody's Dirty Business, Mississippi John Hurt/ Vanguard 19/20,
Historical Records #17
Number Three Blues, Buddy Boy Hawkins/ Yazoo L.1010
On My Last Go Round, Joe Callicott/ Blue Horizon 7-63227
Outside Woman Blues, Blind Joe Reynolds/ Origin of Jazz Library
Parchman Farm Blues, Booker "Bukka" White/ CBS 52629,
Sonet 609
Pay Day, Mississippi John Hurt/ Vanguard 19032
Pea Vine Blues, Charlie Patton/ Yazoo L.1001
Pistol Blues, Bo Weavil Jackson/ Yazoo L.1013
Police Dog Blues, Blind Blake/ Yazoo L.1012
Police Sergeant Blues, Robert Wilkins/ Historical Records
ASC 5829-22
Pony Blues, Charlie Patton/ Yazoo L.1020
Pony Blues, Son House/ Herwin Records
Poor Me, Charlie Patton/ Yazoo L.1020
Preachin' the Blues, Son House/ Origin of Jazz Library,
CBS 62604
Ramblin' On My Mind, Robert Johnson/ CBS 62456, CBS 64102
Revenue Man Blues, Charlie Patton/ Yazoo L.1020
Richland Women Blues, Mississippi John Hurt/ Vanguard 19/20,
Vanguard 79248
Risin' River Blues, George Carter/ Yazoo L.1012
Roberta Blues, Lil Son Jackson/ Arhoolie F.1004
Rolling Stone, Robert Wilkins/ Roots Records
Salty Dog, Mississippi John Hurt/ Vanguard 19/20
Screamin' and Hollerin' the Blues, Charlie Patton/ Yazoo L.1020
See See Rider, Mississippi John Hurt/ Vanguard 19/20
See See Rider, Mance Lipscomb/ Arhoolie F.1001
Shake It and Break It, Charlie Patton/ Yazoo L.1020
Shake Mama Shake, Mance Lipscomb/ Arhoolie F.1001
Sic 'Em Dogs On Me, Booker "Bukka" White/ Herwin Records

Sick Bed Blues, Skip James/ Vanguard 79273, Melodeon 7321
Snatch It and Grab It, Buddy Boy Hawkins/ Yazoo L.1010
Special Rider Blues, Son House/ Yazoo L.1009
Special Rider Blues, Skip James/ Yazoo L.1001, Vanguard 79219,
Biograph 12016
Spike Driver's Blues, Mississippi John Hurt/ Folkways —
"An Anthology of American Folk Music" Vanguard 19032
Spoonful Blues, Charlie Patton/ Yazoo L.1020
Stagolee, Mississippi John Hurt/ Vanguard 19/20, Vanguard 79248
Stingy Mama, Blind Boy Fuller/ Phillips Records
Stones In My Pathway, Robert Johnson/ CBS 62456
Strange Place Blues, Booker "Bukka" White/ CBS 52629
Sugar Babe, Mance Lipscomb/ Arhoolie F.1001
Take Me Back Baby, Mance Lipscomb/ Arhoolie F.1026
Terraplane Blues, Robert Johnson/ CBS 62456
Texas Blues, Marshall Owens/ Yazoo L.1016
That's No Way To Get Along, Robert Wilkins/
Origin of Jazz Library
32-20 Blues, Robert Johnson/ CBS 62456
Thousand Woman Blues, Blind Boy Fuller/ Folkways RF202
Tom Rushen Blues, Charlie Patton/ Yazoo L.1020
Travelling Riverside Blues, Robert Johnson/ CBS 62456
Try Me One More Time, Marshall Owens/ Yazoo L.1016
22-20 Blues, Skip James/ Vanguard 79273
Voice Throwin' Blues, Buddy Boy Hawkins/ Yazoo L.1010
Walkin' Blues, Robert Johnson/ CBS 62456
Weeping Willow, Blind Boy Fuller/ Saydisc 143
When You Got a Good Friend, Robert Johnson/ CBS 62456
When Your Way Gets Dark, Charlie Patton/ Yazoo L.1020
Woman Woman Blues, Ishman Bracy/ Origin of Jazz Library #2
You Can't Keep No Brown, Bo Weavil Jackson/
Origin of Jazz Library
You Don't Know My Mind, Joe Callicott/ Blue Horizons 7-63227
You Don't Mean Me No Good, Mance Lipscomb/ Arhoolie F.1017